Praise for *If the Dance Floor Is*

No matter your role in education, Dr. Joe Clark's book is one you want to read. The book takes you on a journey through stories and passionate writing about what kids deserve from educators at all levels. It reminds us of our "why" as educators—why we do what we do. And what we can do to improve our craft. There is nothing fancy or technical to the art of building relationships, being available, listening, and if these are not working, changing the music. It is not only our job but our moral responsibility to help students "find their Santa suits." Recognizing that each student has talents, gifts, and skills that we can help them to display for the world to see is a theme throughout this work. Dr. Joe Clark's writing should encourage others that there are still great educators out there doing what is best for students and helping progress the profession of education in positive ways!

—**Dr. Holly W. Sutherland**, superintendent of Haleyville City Schools (Alabama) and moderator of #ALedchat

The raw vulnerability with impeccable humor and a whole lot of honesty is exactly what Joe has served up for you! If you've ever made a mistake or think you will, then this is a must-read. The lens in which he spins (pun intended) this book is insightfully hilarious!

—**LaVonna Roth**, speaker, author, and chief illuminator of Ignite Your S.H.I.N.E.®

If you are looking for a refreshing perspective on leading and learning from the lens of a superintendent with experience as a professional disc jockey and camp director, you will love *If the Dance Floor Is Empty, Change the Song* by Dr. Joe Clark. Woven through the pages are stories of connection, told with a candor and vulnerability necessary for promoting personal and professional growth. No matter your role in education—superintendent, district leader, principal, or teacher—you will be empowered to keep the music playing, no matter which generation you serve. There is something for everyone in this book!

—**Tamara Letter, MEd**, instructional coach, technology integrator, and author of *A Passion for Kindness*

It's been said that we never know the struggles that someone is going through, so we should treat them kindly always. In *If the Dance Floor Is Empty, Change the Song*, Joe Clark embraces his own vulnerability to share how he reclaimed his story after a traumatic childhood and used his life experiences—and those as a deejay and camp director—to guide his work as a school leader. This book is an often humorous, sometimes melancholy look into what teaching and school leadership is all about. It's a tremendous read that I know you'll enjoy.

—**Thomas C. Murray**, director of innovation of Future Ready Schools® and author of *Personal & Authentic*

Too often in education we overcomplicate things. In *If the Dance Floor Is Empty, Change the Song*, Joe Clark shares captivating stories from his life that will make you literally laugh out loud and fight back tears, and in doing so, gives the reader great practical advice for succeeding in the field of education. I would recommend this book not only to all school administrators but also to anyone in a position to positively impact kids.

—**Ryan McLane**, principal, director of special education, and coauthor of *Your School Rocks . . . So Tell People!*

If the Dance Floor Is Empty, Change the Song is a look into the world of leadership, education, and how to treat students. Dr. Clark writes to inspire teachers, principals, and superintendents to reflect on the mission of being educators while being reminded to enjoy their work. This quick read will help you reflect and smile as Dr. Clark shares meaning and humor in everyday moments.

—**Todd Whitaker**, leading authority on staff motivation, teacher leadership, and principal effectiveness and author of *What Great Teachers Do Differently*

I thoroughly enjoyed reading *If the Dance Floor Is Empty . . .* by Dr. Joe Clark! This is a great book for any educator or administrator to read. His advice, stories, and experiences are authentic and will definitely hit home with anyone who has been in the field!

—**Dr. Bryan Pearlman**, founder and head trainer of Most Valuable Professional Development

A refreshing read for both leaders and educators of all levels! This is the type of read that can rejuvenate a veteran or give new teachers tools to keep their morale and inspiration at their peak. The lessons you learn from this book can carry over throughout the year, even when you don't know if you can.

—**Amber Teamann**, principal of Whitt Elementary in Wylie ISD in Wylie, Texas

If the Dance Floor Is Empty, Change the Song by Joe Clark is a cleverly written book that will not only make you think about how we approach our jobs as educators but make you chuckle out loud. Filled with personal stories, practical examples, on-point illustrations, and golden nuggets of wisdom, this book will be hard for readers to put down.

—**Jimmy Casas**, educator, author, speaker, and leadership coach

If the Dance Floor Is Empty, Change the Song is a book that will leave you smiling and laughing at times. It will also validate your thinking about education. More importantly, it will challenge you to rethink why we serve as educators and what is most important when discussing education and the purpose of schools. This book is filled with scores of reflections on teaching, learning, and leading that are applicable to educators in all roles, especially school leaders.

—**Jeffrey Zoul, EdD**, author, speaker, leadership coach, and president of ConnectEDD

As a newly appointed principal, I found this book witty, insightful, and inspiring. The real-life stories and anecdotes that Dr. Clark provides are relatable to teachers, school managers, and, honestly, anyone in a position of leadership. *If the Dance Floor Is Empty, Change the Song* should be required reading for both new and seasoned school administrators alike. It should be part of every principal's and teacher's motivational tool kit.

—**David Thomas**, principal of St. Gabriel's Special School, Bishopstown, Cork, Ireland

"Great, another leadership book!" That was my first thought when I was asked to read *If the Dance Floor Is Empty, Change the Song*.

Once I read the first few pages I was hooked; I truly wanted to dance. Finally, a leadership book with great advice and a vast amount of humor. Yes, school is serious business. But if you don't laugh and enjoy the experiences, then why even be a school leader? Dr. Joe Clark has created an informative, quick read that gives you relatable and useful information. I truly did laugh out loud at graphics, pie charts, and stories. If you can't relate to this book, then you truly have never danced to a good song or sat back and enjoyed the experience of being a school leader.

—**Jack Berckemeyer**, presenter, author, humorist, and former assistant executive director for the National Middle School Association

A gourmet meal of insight offered up in perfect bite-sized portions. Devour it all at once like I did, or pick it up whenever you begin to doubt your role as a leader and educator in this world.

—**Drew Dudley**, author of *This Is Day One*

IF THE DANCE FLOOR IS EMPTY, CHANGE THE SONG

DR. JOE CLARK

If the Dance Floor Is Empty, Change the Song

A Superintendent's Spin on Making Schools Rock

If the Dance Floor Is Empty, Change the Song: A Superintendent's Spin on Making Schools Rock

This book is available at special discounts when purchased in quantity for educational purposes or as premiums, promotions, or fundraisers. For inquiries and details, contact the publisher at books@daveburgessconsulting.com.

Published by Dave Burgess Consulting, Inc.

San Diego, CA

DaveBurgessConsulting.com

Library of Congress Control Number: 2020939494

Paperback ISBN: 978-1-951600-30-3

Ebook ISBN: 978-1-951600-31-0

Editing and book production by Reading List Editorial

Cover and interior design by Liz Schreiter

TO ALL THOSE EDUCATORS WHO UNDERSTAND THE POWER THEY HAVE TO SAVE CHILDREN

CONTENTS

Introduction 1

PART 1: SCHOOL LEADERSHIP IS MORE THAN SNOW DAYS: ADVICE FOR PRINCIPALS AND SUPERINTENDENTS

1: New Principals, Heed My Advice (Or Not) 23
2: School Leadership Is More Than Snow Days. 57
3: Make Every Day Opening Day 75
4: It's Easy for You. You're Creative: Boards of Education and the 5–0 Vote 83

PART 2: CAMP IS FOR CAMPERS: A STUDENT-CENTERED APPROACH

5: Camp Is for the Campers (and School Is for the Students). 91
6: Of Pencils, Sporks, and Compliance. 103
7: Beyond Content: The Importance of Relationships in Schools. . . 107
8: Data Have Flesh 113

PART 3: GREAT TEACHERS KNOW WHEN TO CUT THE GRASS: ADVICE FOR TEACHERS

9: Great Teachers Know when to Cut the Grass. 121
10: Teachers, Leave the Sarcasm in Vegas 127
11: A Discombobulated Thursday. 131
12: Fumbles Happen, but Great Teachers Stick to the Game Plan . 135
13: *Sound of Music* Teaching: A Thing of the Past 143
14: Advice for Beginning Teachers: Don't Ignore the Signs 149
15: Wanted: Great Teachers *and* Great Employees 153

PART 4: DON'T WRITE THE REVIEW UNTIL YOU WATCH THE MOVIE: ON KINDNESS, COMMUNITY, AND DIVERSITY

16: Choose Kindness: My Message for New Teachers. 161
17: Every Day We Teach Them Well: The Importance of Community. 177
18: Read the Menu or Eat at the Buffet? The Power of Diversity. . . 185

PART FIVE: GET OFF THE COUCH: ADVICE FOR LIVING

19: Get Off the Couch and Other Stories: Advice for Graduates . . 195

20: It's a *Jerry Springer* World. Are You Onstage or in the Audience? 217

21: Lessons from My Sister, a Teacher Who Left Too Soon. 221

22: Reclaiming My Story 227

Acknowledgments 239

About the Author 241

More from Dave Burgess Consulting, Inc. 245

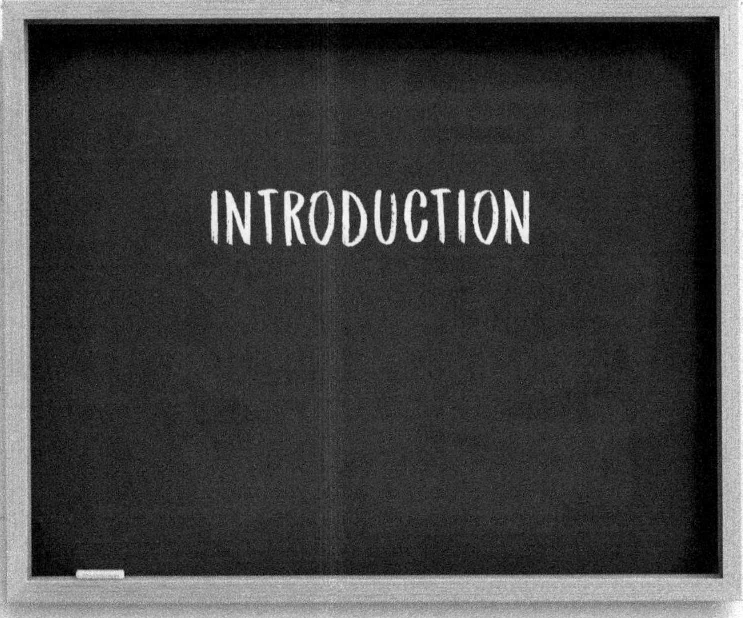

While most college seniors studying to be a teacher learn their most valuable lessons during student teaching, I learned mine in slightly less traditional ways: busting a move, Humpty dancing, and fighting for my right to party. You see, when I was a senior in college, my friend Rich Siebert asked me to help him with his mobile deejay service. I expected to hold the job only until I finished student teaching and found a "real" job. Never did I expect it to turn into a career that would go on for the next twenty-four years, and never did I expect that the lessons I learned would make me a better educator.

Rich had founded Beach Boyz Entertainment a few years prior to my senior year, and his business was starting to grow. I was getting ready to start my student teaching and thought deejaying would be a perfect job. It paid well and was mostly weekend work, and there were worse ways to spend time than playing music and watching people dance.

I told Rich I would help him, and I soon found myself working almost every Friday and Saturday, with plenty of other gigs thrown in. We did weddings, parties, and school dances, and our interactive style and professionalism caused his business to boom. We were innovative for the time, not just playing music but leading dances, clowning around with props, playing games, and interacting with the crowd in various ways.

Over the course of that career, I had many memorable experiences, some pleasant and others not so much. I had the pleasure of deejaying the high school graduation party of Akron native and NBA star LeBron James, and I deejayed parties for NFL quarterbacks Dan Marino and John Elway when they were inducted into the Pro Football Hall of Fame in Canton, Ohio. I also deejayed some wedding receptions where drunken groomsmen threatened to beat me up if I didn't play a certain request and outdoor parties where dogs attacked me or rain drenched my equipment. My favorite gigs were elementary school dances, which were usually about two hours long and involved kids and their parents joining me in all sorts of crazy dances and games. My least favorite gigs: class reunions. Generally, people at class reunions talked more than they danced, and they were typically split down the middle about whether they wanted modern dance music or music from their high school days.

When I graduated from college, I found my first teaching job as a full-time, yearlong substitute English teacher. It didn't pay enough to quit deejaying, so I kept spinning wax. It was a good thing I did. At the end of the year, when the teacher I was subbing for unexpectedly returned, I found myself out of the education game. At that time, a glut of teachers were vying for a shortage of teaching jobs. In fact, the prior year I had been one of only sixteen new teachers hired in all of Summit County. I had plenty of interviews, but the competition was stiff, which had me looking for a job in the business world as well.

Fortunately, late in the summer, I found a full-time English teaching job. A school district I was interviewing with hired a teacher away from another school district in late August. The superintendent who had not hired me still liked me enough to recommend me to the superintendent of the district he had poached his new hire from. Lo and behold, I landed the job. Still, I did not give up my side gig. Rich had too much work and needed the help, and the money I was making went a long way to pay bills. By that time, I was married with a child on the way, and my wife, Amie, and I planned for her to be a stay-at-home mom.

During this same time, I was also working as a day camp director every summer. After teaching for six years, I moved into school administration as a high school assistant principal. I hadn't been looking for a change, but I had finished my licensure and my principal showed me the job posting. Not necessarily wanting the job, I was more candid than I normally would have been in an interview. That candor landed me the position through which I broke into school administration. Being a year-round job, the assistant principalship forced me to give up my day camp job, but with a second child on the way, I was still deejaying every weekend. The business was still growing, and I could think of no other part-time job that could match the pay.

Being a deejay was a pretty great way to build relationships with students. Starting as a teacher and going all the way through my time as a building principal, I had the privilege of deejaying most of our school dances. As I said, the Beach Boyz DJ Service was well known in Northeast Ohio, mainly because we were innovators with being interactive with the crowd. We would teach and lead dances, bring percussion instruments for people to play, and engage the crowd over the microphone. It was really simple stuff, but it worked great.

For example, are you familiar with the song "Shout" by Otis Day & the Knights, the traditional party song that was made popular in the movie *Animal House*? In the middle of the song, after Otis sings, "Now waaaiiit a minute," the song gets quiet for about forty-five seconds. Most deejays will allow the dead air, with maybe someone in the crowd shouting "Yeah! Yeah!" like they did in the movie. But not the Beach Boyz. When it came to the quiet part of the song, I would say over the microphone, "Okay, ladies, it's your turn to scream right now." And the dance hall would fill with screams.

Then I'd say, "Okay, guys, it's your turn." And the guys would scream.

Then, "How about the freshmen?" Screams.

"Sophomores?" More screams.

"Juniors?" Even more screams.

"Seniors?" Ear-piercing screams.

If I was deejaying a wedding, I would follow the same pattern, only the prompts to scream would be different: "How about the friends of the bride? Friends of the groom? Anyone from out of town? How about everyone who wishes the bride and groom the best in their new lives together?" And the place would erupt.

Another favorite was pitting kids against adults, or men against women, or friends of the bride against friends of the groom to see who could most loudly shout and gesture with "Y.M.C.A." at the appropriate times. I didn't realize then that this kind of back-and-forth with the audience helped me develop skills that I would later use in education. When we played "The Twist," we'd make it a contest between men and women, alternating between the men twisting and the women twisting. I would always give bonus points to the team who had somebody dancing extra funky, and I always gave the bride's team bonus points because of how beautiful the bride looked that night. At the end of the contest I would announce that, after the 894 wedding receptions I had deejayed, the ladies remained undefeated. Introducing competition helped build the energy in the room and always filled the dance floor.

To start a wedding reception off, I'd announce that only people who loved the bride and groom were invited onto the dance floor. "If you have ill feelings toward the bride and groom and hope this marriage doesn't quite work out, please stay seated," I would say.

"Otherwise, please join the bride and groom on the floor for the first dance of the night." The dance floor was always packed from song one. That was a moment of building consensus—and later I realized I could also use this in my professional life.

At every gig, I would go out onto the floor and lead a few dances. I can't count how many people I taught the electric slide, the macarena, the cha-cha slide, and the Cupid shuffle to as each dance became a flash in the world of pop culture. I was most known for teaching silly dance steps like the water sprinkler, the pencil sharpener, the flight attendant, the lawn mower, and more during the song "The Bird" by the Time. Kids who had me as their English teacher or assistant principal were shocked to see that Mr. Clark knew a lot about music and had some pretty dope moves.

I remember one time when deejaying a homecoming dance for our school as a teacher, I was excited to show off our newest prop, a carbon dioxide–propelled confetti launcher. My deejay table was in the corner of the gymnasium, and the dance floor was packed. When it came time to introduce the homecoming court, kids swarmed around an aisle that went from the entrance of the gym to a stage on the opposite side. Through the crowd, I could see the heads of the court walking down the aisle as I introduced them to the theme of *2001: A Space Odyssey*. The gym had a huge canopy draped from the ceiling. To shoot the confetti, I had to aim above the crowd's heads but under the canopy. I announced the king and queen and waited for them to reach the middle of the aisle, where I was prepared to shower them with confetti. Unfortunately, I did not realize the confetti bomb had a fastener I was supposed to remove to allow the confetti to explode into a massive cloud of colored paper squares.

The good news is my aim was absolutely perfect.

The bad news is I shot the homecoming queen directly in the side of her face with a giant wad of confetti. We laughed about it later. The incident also taught me to apologize and take responsibility for things going wrong, a skill I've come to rely on often in my career.

From these kinds of experiences, I began to understand how my deejay skills could help me as a teacher. I learned to read the energy of the room—or lack thereof. I developed the confidence to manage a large group. I became comfortable speaking in public. And I learned what to do when people were not having a good time.

As I continued to deejay, my educational career continued to advance. When I was promoted from high school assistant principal after three years to middle school principal, I was adamant I was going to stop deejaying. No such luck. Like a member of Don Corleone's family, every time I tried to get out, I was pulled back in. Frankly, I was pretty good. The Beach Boyz got many, many requests from clients for me to be their deejay, and the company implemented a policy that increased my pay even more if I was specifically requested.

I was a middle school principal for four years before moving into the central office as assistant superintendent, at which time I started my doctoral program. It didn't matter, though; the deejay life kept a hold on me. Beach Boyz Entertainment kept winning the annual "*Beacon*'s Best" for its deejay service, an award voted on by the readership of the *Akron Beacon Journal*, and the work never stopped.

Finally, after six years as an assistant superintendent in three different districts, I became a superintendent and cut the deejay ropes. Sort of. I still had a handful of clients who requested me, but I scaled my work way back until the year came when I did zero gigs. In total, the part-time job I thought would last for a year lasted twenty-four.

I continued to draw on the skills I learned in my side jobs as a deejay and camp director because they helped me thrive as a teacher, principal, and superintendent. Many of the activities I used interacting with large groups of people could be applied in my school jobs, either with student lessons or teacher professional development or parent programs. Both side gigs also helped develop my leadership abilities, my sense of creativity, and my innovation in finding solutions to problems and deciding on approaches to daily tasks.

I am a huge introvert, which sounds strange coming from a person who has spent so much of his life on stage deejaying or speaking in front of students and campers. But in many ways, I see my work as performance, and I am much more comfortable being on stage in front of four thousand people than I am mingling at a party with four people. I tend to be an observer, and my observations lead me to reflect on the connections between my community and my current role as a school leader. Over my years in the deejay business, I made certain observations, namely that deejaying and education have a lot more in common than people realize. A mediocre deejay can stand behind his table and play music and have a relatively average career. A great one realizes that deejaying is more than playing music: it is interaction, creativity, and service. It is being vulnerable enough to recognize when the performance is not going well and having the confidence to switch midstream. Deejaying is not simply playing music, just as teaching is not simply standing and delivering lessons. In the following pages, I share some of my collected observations about how the skills I learned as a deejay can apply to our school communities.

If the Dance Floor Is Empty, Change the Song

As much as you might want to stand around blaming the crowd for being boring, that's not going to fill the dance floor. What *will* fill the dance floor is playing great music and interacting with the crowd. The same is true in the classroom. If kids are not engaged in a lesson, complaining about their lack of motivation is not going to solve the problem. Instead, differentiate your instruction to motivate each individual student. A huge part of this idea is choice and authenticity. Students are much more likely to stay on the dance floor if the music is interesting to them.

I left the classroom in 1998, and things were much different back then. We had no common curriculum and no standards. I did not have a computer in my classroom, and my walls had literal blackboards on them. At that point in my career, I was expected to teach the textbook and follow the methods of the more senior teachers in the English department. But even back then I recognized that my students needed choice in determining which novels they would read and what topics they would write about. I knew that my students were much more likely to be engaged if the work assigned was authentic. For instance, my English Olympics unit, in which teams of students competed in a variety of English language arts activities, was a hit because team members selected activities based on their strengths and interests. Activities ranged from The Great Mail Race, in which students practiced their business letter writing skills by soliciting donations we could use in the classroom from companies around the world, to All the World's a Stage, in which students wrote and then performed a one-act play.

All students were also required to write a research paper, and my department chairperson was disgusted with me when I did not require my students to use note cards. This might sound dated because I was in the classroom so long ago, but back in the day, kids had to do their research using print materials, such as books and scholarly journals. As the students researched, they were to copy notes from the materials, verbatim, onto note cards. I never understood the reasoning. I had just graduated college with an English degree, and in the volumes of things I had written, never once had I copied notes from a source to a note card. I just used highlighters.

So I fought back against the English department chairperson, arguing that the task we were giving our students—making the note cards—was not authentic. I insisted that never again would my students use such an outdated and arbitrary process. And do you know what happened? My students wrote some fantastic research papers, on topics of their choosing, using the organizational processes most comfortable to them.

Now, as a superintendent twenty years removed from teaching, I visit classrooms often and see outstanding teachers who have mastered the practices of choice and authenticity. Students are solving real problems, answering real questions, and having a say in the work they do. Yet every once in a blue moon, I visit a classroom where all the kids are doing the same task the same way, maybe doing a work sheet where they are regurgitating information, and I see them begging the teacher to change the song.

Nobody Will Remember the Chicken or Rigatoni or Green Beans, but They Will Remember If They Had a Good Time

Every wedding is on a budget, and tough choices need to be made. We used to remind brides and grooms that in thirty years nobody will remember what they ate, but they will remember if they had fun at your wedding.

In the same way, thirty years from now most students will not necessarily remember the history or math or science lesson you taught them, but they will remember how you made them feel. Therefore, building relationships should be a top priority for teachers. Kids don't care what you know until they know you care.

When I was a middle school principal, Scotty was the kind of eighth grader that led some principals to early retirement. He was fidgety, sarcastic, smart, devious, always into some sort of trouble, likely to cut class or refuse to do work, a believer that rules were merely suggestions—exactly the kind of student I loved. Yes, he was mischievous. Yes, he was goofy. Yes, he was just like me when I was in eighth grade.

Scotty lived next door to my secretary, Jayne. One spring morning, we were surprised that Scotty and his two best friends, the twins, were absent from school. Students like Scotty are never absent from school. They are the kind of student teachers wish would be absent but never are.

Except this day. Scotty and the twins were absent, which was unusual enough for us to have a conversation about it in the office. Jayne said, "Well, he was outside waving to me this morning when I was getting in my car. He was putting something in the back of his dad's truck."

Weird.

"And the twins were with him," Jayne said.

Weirder yet.

The day went on, and time for lunch duty came upon me. As I was talking to the students eating lunch, one of the boys told me how excited he was to go to Silver Creek Park after school. This was the day that Silver Creek stocked the lake with trout.

"What did you say?" I asked.

"Yeah," he said. "They stock the lake with trout. It's awesome."

And the lightbulb over my head suddenly turned on.

Our school had an outdoor education program. Every year we would take all the seventh graders camping for three days in the beautiful Cuyahoga Valley National Park. It was a great program, and the kids participated in all sorts of outdoor activities they may not have normally had the opportunity to do. I made my way to the closet where we kept all of our camping supplies and grabbed myself a fishing rod.

Soon I was in my car heading to Silver Creek Park. As I drove on the long driveway, I could see across the lake to where Scotty and the twins were standing at the end of the pier, fishing for trout.

I parked my car, grabbed the fishing rod, and made my way down the crowded pier. People were whispering among themselves as they watched me, dressed in a suit and tie, walk slowly to the end of the pier. I stood just behind the boys, who had lines cast and a five-gallon bucket full of the day's catch.

I cast my line into the pond, and then loud enough for the boys to hear, I said, "Anything biting?"

You could have knocked them over with a stick.

I told the boys to pack up their gear and come with me. As we walked back toward the parking lot, I could hear people chuckling and taunting the kids: "You guys got busted!"

We got to my car, and the boys asked if they could at least keep the fish they caught. I said yes, and Scotty put the five-gallon bucket of trout between his legs in the front seat as I drove them back to school. When we got to school, I put the bucket of fish in our cafeteria cooler so the boys could take their catch home with them.

I assigned the boys a day of in-school suspension, mainly so they could make up the work they missed. And as I walked them to the ISS room, one of the twins said, "Mr. Clark, I forgot that I have this . . ." And he pulled out a giant hunting knife. I told him to come get it in my office after the day was done.

I tell that story often and am often met with disbelief that I let the kids off so easily. After all, they were truant from school, and they had a weapon.

Honestly, I thought it was one of the most refreshing things I have seen in my career. They were fishing. They could have been out doing drugs, or breaking into cars, or any sort of other horrible things, but they were just fishing. Outside. At the park. Having fun. Feeding their families. And, I'm guessing, learning more than they might have in school that day. The fact that they knew the park was stocking the pond with trout shows a level of civic engagement that many people—kids or adults—never reach.

That day I had a choice. I could punish the kids severely and give them another reason to not like school. Or I could show empathy and understanding, recognize their great catch, and remember that some crimes really aren't meant to be severely punished.

A few years later, I ran into Scotty. He was working at a gas station where I popped in to buy a soda. He recognized me instantly, and we talked about that day. He still remembered it and was still grateful that I had treated him kindly. He was almost finished with his bachelor's degree, and he thanked me for making middle school tolerable for him.

There Are Two Kinds of People in the World: Those Who Like Barry Manilow and Those Who Pretend They Don't Like Barry Manilow

If you pass out a few maracas and tambourines and play "Copacabana" at a wedding reception, chances are you will have a huge conga line dancing throughout the hall. And for those who aren't in the conga line—those who are sitting down pretending they hate the song—look closely at their feet. I bet you anything they are tapping them and humming along.

There are a lot of egos involved in education, particularly with students. Nobody likes to be embarrassed in front of peers, especially kids. Sometimes kids will pretend not to be interested in participating in school because it might seem uncool. The savvy teacher will recognize these kids—the closet Barry Manilow lovers—and find ways to keep them engaged in learning while allowing them to maintain their image.

Larry was one of those kids for me. He was the stereotypical "stoner," never coming to class prepared, often with his head down. He was not disruptive other than through passive defiance. Larry just did not want to participate in class, never had his materials, and appeared apathetic to an objective observer. When I collected assignments, Larry liked to make everyone aware that he hadn't done his, and he would put his head down and feign a nap.

But Larry and I had a little secret. He always did all of his assigned work and stayed after class to hand it in, pulling it out of his pants pocket and unfolding it before passing it to me. Larry was a great writer and a lover of literature. But he also loved that his classmates thought he was a goof-off, and he worked hard to sell that image. I didn't care. I knew Larry was learning, and it was not worth fighting a battle over some perceived lack of discipline in my classroom.

If You Play Neil Diamond's "Sweet Caroline" Near the End of Dinner and Nobody Sings Along, It's Going to Be a Long Night

I used to call "Sweet Caroline" my barometer song. I always played it near the end of dinner, when conversations started picking up, as a test to see if it was going to be a fun night. Invariably, if people sang along—especially to the iconic "BAH BAH BAH!"s—it was almost always a great wedding reception. But if nobody sang along, it seemed like those wedding receptions dragged, even though I'd change the song throughout the night.

In the same way, if you don't hook kids in the first days of the school year, it's going to be a long year. Spending the first days of school in August teaching kids the rules *will not* prevent them from breaking the rules in April. Spending the first days of school in August building relationships and trust with students *will* prevent them from breaking rules in April. It goes back to three things: relationships, relationships, relationships. The tone is set at the beginning of the year, and it's hard to recover if the tone that's set is negative.

As a teacher, I would set aside the first few days of class—but not to go over rules and procedures. The kids were being inundated with rules and procedures from all their other teachers anyway, so what was the likelihood they would remember anything I told them? Instead, we spent days doing different icebreakers and name-learning games. I modeled for them how they could expect me to treat them and how I expected them to treat each other. And I had them working, giving them early chances to see some success, especially in their writing.

As a superintendent, I try to stress the same thing with our teachers and staff. At new-teacher orientation, we talk a lot about the expectations for how we treat kids. And at our convocation day, to which all employees are invited, we spend literally zero time talking about test scores. Instead, we set the tone with student performances, sometimes the band playing, sometimes the choir singing. We sing the alma mater together. Sometimes new kindergarten parents will speak to the staff about the fears they are facing with their first child heading off to school. Sometimes students speak, thanking the staff for the positive influence they have had on their life.

I even share about my summer, making sure to poke fun at myself for some crazy thing I did. For example, one summer I found a Cheetos cheese puff that looked like a running man, and I got it accepted into the official Cheetos Museum. Another year, I talked about how I did a stand-up comedy routine on a cruise ship. Another time, I told about my adventure in Florida witnessing a police-involved shooting, which, believe it or not, had a humorous twist. These stories are not pointless time fillers. Everything I do and say has a purpose. Instead of talking about the gloom and doom of state testing, starting the year with laughter sets the tone that our jobs are fun, that we are a family that laughs together so that the times we cry are not as devastating.

The bottom line is that we intentionally spend time talking about relationships and little about the actual work. There is time for work talk later. As we begin the year, I want to make sure we take time to recommit to the mission of serving kids.

A Bride Goes to a Reception Only Once, but a Deejay Goes to a Thousand Receptions

Brides are nervous. They want a perfect wedding, and they are counting on everyone involved to give it to them. Because a bride gets married only once but a deejay goes to a thousand weddings, it is up to the deejay to take control, guide the bride and groom through the reception, and make them feel confident that it will be the best day of their lives.

Kids (and usually their parents) go through your class only once, but you teach the grade or class for thirty-five years. They are nervous and don't know what to expect. Your job, like the deejay's, is to ease their anxiety.

How? Communication.

It's imperative that you engage your students and their parents in constant communication; you need email, Twitter, and even the telephone in your toolbox. The telephone is the most underused type of educational technology today. Make the call home; nothing is more powerful in reducing anxiety than hearing the voice of another human being.

I will never forget my first year of teaching. I had decided to make a habit of calling five parents per week to tell them how awesome their child was doing in my class. When one mother answered her phone and heard my good news about her daughter, she started crying. She said that her sister—the student's aunt—had passed away the day before, and hearing from me was a bright spot during this horrible time.

We all love hearing people brag about our own children. Why are we so reluctant to brag about other people's children to their parents? It costs nothing but time, and the rewards are immense. These moments are so important for helping students and parents calm their anxieties, so taking that time to make a phone call can really pay off.

As you can maybe tell, I loved working as a mobile deejay. And I love working as an educator even more. But truth be told, deejaying taught me a lot about being a better educator. That is why I wrote this book. Thousands of great books about education are out there, written by brilliant educators. Classroom teachers, principals, superintendents—I've even read a book or two written by a bus driver—provide great insight into education from within the field. But I also want you to see that educators can learn to be better by looking at their own work through a different lens. My other work as a deejay and camp director has given me so many unique insights into what education and leadership are all about.

I've organized this collection of essays by theme. And interspersed throughout the book are flowcharts, calendars, Venn diagrams, and other graphic organizers. You will find the essays to be mostly introspective and thoughtful, sometimes humorous, and often connected to the world of education, leadership, or work with children. They represent the ego and superego of me and most school leaders, people who recognize the huge responsibility of creating school cultures in which children feel safe and thrive academically, socially, and emotionally. Part 1 offers leadership advice for principals and superintendents. Part 2 discusses how to keep the focus on students in our work. Part 3 offers advice for teachers, while part 4 focuses on kindness, community, and diversity. Finally, part 5 is my advice for living, both inside and outside of the world of education.

The graphics included are tongue in cheek, sometimes irreverent, often sarcastic glimpses into the world of schools. They are the id. These items are steeped in reality but shown through a bit of a snarky lens. These are the kinds of things school people talk to their colleagues about in the secrecy of faculty lounges or job-alike meetings to help us cope with the immense pressure of our jobs. We do serious work every day—life-changing work—but the best school people do not take themselves too seriously. We laugh so we don't cry, and we see funny things in our work almost daily.

When I was deejaying, I sometimes felt that people viewed me with an air of arrogance. I was "just a deejay" after all, some schlep making his living spinning wax on the weekends. This attitude became clear every so often with how some people treated me, not unlike someone in a restaurant acting superior to the waitstaff. I often wondered if people would treat me differently if they knew I was a school principal or assistant superintendent or superintendent, with three college degrees.

The truth is it shouldn't matter. One does not need credentials to lead well, interact with others well, or treat children well. As you sit down to read this book, remember that inspiration can come from anywhere, even from a mobile disc jockey. I also hope you will find this book as enjoyable to read as I did to write. If you don't, put the book down. After all, if the dance floor is empty, change the song.

School Administrator Skills

COVERED IN GRADUATE SCHOOL STUDIES	ACTUALLY USED IN REAL LIFE
Structure and Organization of Public Education	Judging the Faculty Chili Cook-Off without Hurting the Losers' Feelings
Systems for Observing and Analyzing Instruction	Making Sense of Ambiguous Weather Forecasts
Foundations in Educational Administration	Stopping Girl Fights without Causing Trouble for Yourself
Organizational Behavior in Education	Refraining from Using Sarcasm When Sarcasm Is Definitely Called For
Designing In-Service Education Programs	Apologizing for Things That Are Not Your Fault
Culture, Gender, and Race in Organizations	Looking Interested at the Second Grade Recorder Concert
Systems of Human Inquiry	Giving Teachers a Less Than Perfect Evaluation without Making Them Cry
Ethics and Values in Educational Administration	Keeping Four Hundred Students from Freaking Out during a Power Outage
Institutional Analysis and Planning	Motivating Employees without Being Able to Promote or Give Raises
Managing Instructional Resources	Discovering Loopholes in State Regulations

{PART 1}

SCHOOL LEADERSHIP IS MORE THAN SNOW DAYS:

Advice for Principals and Superintendents

—1—

NEW PRINCIPALS, HEED MY ADVICE (OR NOT)

Many teachers will be hired over the summer into their first job as principal. They likely have completed countless hours of rigorous coursework, researched and written many papers, and completed an internship with an accomplished principal. They have probably seen some principals make decisions they disagreed with and have vowed to do it differently when given their chance, and they likely have had some great role models, too.

Chances are those folks making the transition from the classroom to the office are not sleeping well over the summer. Their minds are racing with ideas, and they are being inundated by introductions to new people, all of whom have an agenda they are promoting, for good or bad. These new principals will learn something very quickly: graduate school did not prepare them for this.

But grad school was important. They needed it to get their credentials to work as a school administrator, and their law class was probably very insightful. Still, they will spend a lot of time at the school of hard knocks, learning on the job. Here are some things I wish someone had told me when I became a school administrator.

The Five Words You Must Learn to Say Are "I'm Sorry. I Was Wrong."

If you want to be a successful administrator, you must learn to say five simple words: "I'm sorry. I was wrong." I can promise you only one thing: you are going to mess up. When you do, don't hide from your mistake or blame others. Admit it. Apologize to those you hurt. Do everything you can to make things better. And try not to make the same mistake again.

I learned this lesson on January 24, 2013, one of the worst days of my professional life. I remember sitting in my car in the parking garage of the Ohio Elections Commission, sobbing like a baby out of stress and fear. I was about to appear in front of a group of people who had the power to fine me, imprison me, and remove my license as an Ohio educator.

But let me go back and set the scene.

I was named acting superintendent of the Nordonia Hills City School District on November 1, 2011. On November 8, the voters of our community passed a levy that saved us from the brink of financial disaster. The levy, though, only stopped the bleeding. Our financial forecast showed that we needed to be on the ballot again soon or we would be in dire straits again.

Sure enough, the board of education placed on the November 2012 ballot a small levy, which failed miserably. The levy committee, the Friends of Nordonia Schools, had drained its coffers over the previous two years in six levy attempts. I was a rookie superintendent, overwhelmed by not only the stress of being new to my position but also of having to cut staff and programs. I was blindly following the example that had been set. We needed more money if we were going to run another campaign, so three days after the vote, I fired off an email to our staff, not unlike the emails I had heard of other superintendents in other districts sending many times before. I wrote:

> Dear Nordonia Staff:
>
> With the recent failure of Issue 65, there will be a need for the district to be on the ballot for another levy, possibly as soon as November 2013. Unfortunately, this past campaign drained the funds of the Friends of Nordonia Schools.
>
> Will you please consider a donation to the Friends through payroll deduction? If a sizable portion of our staff donated $3 per pay period, we will be prepared to run another campaign in a year without having to worry about doing massive fundraising efforts. With an organized opposition group now formed, your support is needed now more than ever.
>
> I know times are tough for everybody, and I understand if you are not able to do this at this time. Thanks in advance for your consideration.
>
> Joe Clark, PhD
> Superintendent
> Nordonia Hills City Schools

After sending the email, I attended the Ohio School Boards Association Capital Conference—the state's annual conference for school board members and administrators—from November 11 through November 14 in Columbus. While at the conference, in conversation with our board attorneys, I learned that soliciting political contributions from public employees was precluded by Ohio law.

Realizing that my correspondence on November 9 to the Nordonia Hills staff was potentially inappropriate and could be construed as a possible violation of election law, I sent a second email to the employees immediately upon returning from Columbus on the evening of November 14, admitting I'd made a mistake. I offered my deepest apologies and asked the staff to disregard my request.

I thought that was the end of it, that I had learned my lesson and it was over.

However, after the Thanksgiving holiday, the leader of the newly formed antilevy political action committee, euphemistically named Citizens for Strong Nordonia Schools, filed a complaint with the Ohio Elections Commission alleging violations of election law. A few days later, the executive director of the commission issued a notice stating that the matter had been scheduled for preliminary review on January 24, 2013.

In preparation for the hearing, I submitted a statement for the commission's consideration. In the statement, I admitted to sending the email asking for donations, I admitted learning a few days later that I should not have asked for donations, and I admitted retracting the email and apologizing for my oversight. I also stated that it was not my intent to violate the law, but I accepted responsibility for my lapse in judgment. I ended the statement by saying that I would defer to the wisdom of the commission in determining next steps.

So there I was in tears, parked in the Ohio Elections Commission parking garage for the January review. I grew up Catholic, which means guilt is a big part of my DNA. Here I was, clearly in violation of the law, a law that carried a fine, a six-month prison sentence, and that undoubtedly would put an end to my job and my good reputation with my family and the community.

When I met with the committee, my crying didn't stop. I'm glad they did not record the hearing, because I have never been so embarrassed in my life. The stress of all that was going on caused me to break. I could barely say more than "I'm sorry."

A few weeks later, I got a letter in the mail from the Ohio Elections Commission, which I tore open immediately. It stated that they did find a violation, but for "good cause shown," they would "not impose a fine or refer the matter for further prosecution." The letter also informed me that the commission required no further action of me.

I breathed a sigh of relief and reflected on what I had learned.

I was angry with myself for making the mistake to begin with. I was a new superintendent, so I should have done more research before sending the email. But I was also proud. I was proud that I had the courage to admit I was wrong and to apologize for my mistake. Too often we read about leaders who exponentially worsen a situation by attempting a cover-up more so than by committing the offense itself.

Over the next few months, the small group of residents in the antischool PAC wrote letters to the editor of our widely read local paper, *The News Leader*, asking the board to discipline me for my "crime." But the board stood with me, as did many other residents who wrote letters in my support. Fortunately, nobody expects anybody to be perfect. The best thing we can do when we mess up is admit it, make it right, and move on. Being willing to show vulnerability in our fallibility does wonders for building credibility and trust with the community.

That story might be a more extreme circumstance than one you'd ever encounter, but here's a more likely scenario, especially if you live in the Midwest or Northeast. In my part of Ohio, weather is unpredictable. They say if you don't like the weather, just wait a few hours. It will change.

Starting in December, or November, or sometimes even October, superintendents find themselves on snow-day alert. We check the weather constantly, and if it looks like roads may be dangerous the next day, we set our alarms for about 4:00 a.m. so we can drive the streets the next morning to determine if we need to delay or cancel school for the day.

The best kind of snow day is the no-brainer. We already know the night before that we need to close the schools. When the weather calls for such clear action, we call snow days around dinnertime the night before so parents can make childcare arrangements for the next day. But those days are few and far between.

More often, Ohio weather conditions vary like crazy within a short time and within the predictions themselves. It may be forty degrees in the evening, with a chance for temperatures to drop overnight and a 15 to 99 percent likelihood of snow ranging from a dusting to ten inches. Or it might be that the weather is expected to be fine until about eight in the morning and then turn awful. Or maybe it is supposed to be good weather until ten, turn awful for a couple of hours, then be fine again later in the afternoon.

Why does all this matter? Because each of our bus routes has three runs, with our school start times ranging from about seven to nine. Morning buses are on the road as early as 6:00 a.m. and as late as 9:30 a.m. So if snow is expected at eight, that means about half of our students will already be safe at school when the snow starts. But that puts the other half of our students at risk. If the snow is not supposed to start until ten and is expected to last only a few hours, we could conceivably get everyone to school and back home safely, with the roads being dangerous only during the hours the kids are in class.

Sometimes it is easy work: we are supposed to get ten inches of snow, it starts falling the night before, never lets up, and the roads are impassable in the morning when the decision needs to be made. And sometimes it is more difficult: I wake up at four in the morning to dry roads. The weather calls for a storm to move in around nine, but it could be a little earlier, or it could miss our area entirely. Those are the stressful mornings. Still, most parents understand the difficulty in weighing all the factors for making the decision to close school.

Sometimes, I just drop the ball. The weather forecast is good, so I do not set my alarm to get up early. And by the time I wake up, after the first buses are already on the road, I find the forecast has changed and snow is due shortly or already falling.

One such day was January 9, 2015. The overnight forecast called for dropping temperatures, but snow was not supposed to start falling until after school had started in all our buildings. When I woke up around 5:30 a.m., snow was falling lightly and the forecast showed the heavy stuff not arriving until later in the morning. Buses would be on the road by six, and it was clear to me that travel would be safe.

But I live in Ohio, where the weather can turn bad faster than milk in the sun. By seven, the wind had picked up and we found ourselves in whiteout conditions for the next several hours. Several neighboring school districts had played it safe and closed, making our district one of the few open in the area. My Twitter account started getting hammered with tweets from angry students and parents. Voicemail after voicemail appeared in my inbox. I listened to them on my way to work. As you might imagine, none were complimentary.

So what did I do? I made my way to work, sat down at my desk, and wrote an apology (with the heading "What Was I Thinking?") that I emailed to all the parents and staff. I gave the reasons for my decision, apologized that it was the wrong one, and asked their forgiveness. And I called back every person who left a voicemail and let them criticize me for the bad decision. I ended each call with an apology and a promise to try to do better next time.

Many superintendents in that same situation become defensive. After all, it is Ohio weather, which we all know can change at any time. Also, parents do have the right to keep their kids home from school if they feel transportation will be unsafe. But being defensive is an unwise way to go. It only makes people angrier. And trying to convince people against their will is not really convincing them at all.

When I interviewed for my job, I told the board of education that I would make only one promise: I will screw up. I also told the board that when I did, I would admit it, apologize for it, make reparations when needed, and try better next time.

In this case, when I could have justified my decision because of fickle weather, I knew that the best course of action was simply to apologize. Winning an argument is not always winning, especially if it is going to cause damage to a relationship.

Sadly, apologizing is so rare that people are often taken aback by it. When somebody calls and starts yelling about something they are angry about, a simple "I'm so sorry you are having a bad experience with us" does wonders to disarm them, which then allows us to get to the root of the problem and search for a solution. It is not helpful to say "It's not my fault" or "You are wrong to be angry" or to be defensive in any other way.

I have found over the years that I have spent a great deal of my time apologizing, often for things that are not my fault. When a parent calls angry over something a teacher said to their student, before I even begin to investigate the truth of the matter, the first words out of my mouth usually are "I am so sorry you are having a bad experience with us. I want every student and every parent to be satisfied, and clearly we missed the mark."

Those words are not untrue. I really am sorry they are having a bad experience. Nor does it sell out the teacher. I am not admitting the teacher did anything wrong without first investigating. But something clearly made this parent angry, and I am truly sorry they are feeling this way.

Something else happens when you apologize. Besides defusing an angry person, you build trust. That angry person is going to hang up the phone, and their spouse is going to ask, "What did he say?" And the angry person is going to say, "He said he was sorry." And when they go to parties or talk to people at church or the grocery store and the topic of the schools comes up, they will have a story to tell about how you apologized and how much they respect you for that. And the community's level of trust in you will rise.

Never Underestimate the Power of the Popsicle

It's one of my favorite days of the summer. Every year, the high school administrative team and I stop at the grocery store, buy 180 Popsicles, and take them to our students and chaperones at band camp.

We want the band to know how much we support them and how important they are to the district. A high school band is one of the greatest ambassadors for a school, and it is not always given the appreciation it deserves for the spirit it brings to games, parades, and other community events. And, quite honestly, the gratitude and support the band kids and parents show us is amazing, simply because we do something a little unexpected like buying and delivering a frozen treat. We might spend about fifty dollars out of our pockets, but the return we get in terms of trust and positive relationship building is priceless.

My advice to school leaders everywhere is this: when it comes to earning community trust, don't underestimate the power of the Popsicle. The most successful leaders are those that do the unexpected. In his book *The Greatest Miracle in the World*, Og Mandino says, "The only certain means of success is to render more and better service than is expected of you, no matter what your task may be."

People expect school administrators to attend football and basketball games. Of course, school administrators will also be at open house and graduation and probably even the spring choir concert and the school musical or play. These are the sorts of events where school administrators would be more conspicuous by their absence than attendance, and they would likely hear community rumblings if they did not show up. Obviously, you will go to the varsity football game; parents expect that. After all, football brings in a large crowd of not only parents but many other community members.

But parents do not expect you to deliver Popsicles to band camp for the students who put in every bit of time and hard work as the football team and who are so often overlooked. Going to events that people do not expect you to attend is where a school administrator can gain a lot of community trust. It shows that the administrator values all students and all programs. The community becomes aware of and is grateful for the long hours you are working.

Don't have a band? Then, on the last day of school before winter break, hand out cookies to kids as they enter the building. Or appear in the talent show. Or dress up on Halloween. Or go to the bowling team's match or the mock trial team's competition.

In other words, do the unexpected. You will not gain support by doing the things that are expected of you. But when you do the unexpected, kids and parents see that you are human and you care, and they are more willing to forgive you when you mess up.

I can't count the number of times I attended a "fringe" event in my career, only to find that I am the only school administrator in the house. This is almost always the case when I attend competitions for our mock trial and Science Olympiad teams. My other school administrators and I are almost always the only school leaders at state competitions for band and at solo and ensemble competitions for band and choir. In our area, our students frequently win art contests, yet we never see administrators from other schools in attendance.

Obviously, the purpose of attending these events is to show support for the students. But the nice side benefit is that the parents in attendance are often shocked to see us, and they go home and tell their neighbors (or post on social media) how impressed they were to see us there, sometimes commenting that we've given up our own family time on a weekend to support their kids.

The same is true for fringe sports. Almost every high school administrator and superintendent goes to varsity football and basketball games at home. Turning up at an away game is surprising. Even more unpredictable is going to the cross-country meet or the hockey game late on a Sunday night. I have never seen another school administrator at a golf or tennis match, but I have seen parents there who are grateful for the support. Parents whose kids are normally overlooked get to feel special, and they share that special feeling with their friends and neighbors. The community takes note that you are invested, adding credibility chips to your pile.

So naturally you're wondering, "How do I find time to attend all these events?"

My answer? "You make it."

One thing all of us have in common with Thomas Edison, Martin Luther King Jr., and Mother Teresa is that we all have twenty-four hours in a day. It is a matter of spending time on what you value. If you value supporting your students and strengthening relationships with parents and the community, you find a way to get it done. This brings me back to my point about having the sincerity necessary to do the work to gain community support. If you do not buy into the

ONE THING ALL OF US HAVE IN COMMON WITH THOMAS EDISON, MARTIN LUTHER KING JR., AND MOTHER TERESA IS THAT WE ALL HAVE TWENTY-FOUR HOURS IN A DAY.

value you *give* by going to as many events as you can manage, you will never reap the value you *gain* by putting in the time.

In other words, if you're thinking, "I'm going to the tennis match so the parents will see me," don't bother going. You will end up bitter about giving up the time you put in for such a small gain. The value comes one step at a time, and it takes years to build your reputation as someone who supports even the kids participating in the less popular activities. To make this time investment work without burning yourself out, you first have to want to be there for the kids. It is this servant-leadership mentality that makes going to the events actually enjoyable, which makes your job fun and seem almost not like work, which allows you the patience to slowly reap the side benefits of strengthening your relationship of trust with the community.

I have heard the excuses: I have a family. I have to watch my kids. I have to let my dog out. Whatever the reason, if you place a value on attending school events, you will find a way to do it. Maybe it means bringing your kids or your dog along. Maybe it means sharing your Saturdays and Sundays. Or maybe it means pulling the occasional late night stacking events (e.g., depending on where the games are, I can hit middle school volleyball, then high school tennis, volleyball, and soccer, all on the same night). It is not necessary to stay for the entire event, but spend enough time to make it meaningful.

It takes a ton of work and a ton of time. But if you are a new administrator who can find ways to render more and better service than is expected, you are much more likely to build trust and grow relationships within the community that help ensure your success. Kids and parents connecting with you in a meaningful way also means they will be more willing to forgive you when your performance is less than stellar.

Err on the Side of the Kid

You will have to make really tough decisions. And in almost every decision you have to make, you will be lobbied in a bunch of different ways by a bunch of different people. So when the time comes to make the decision, you can't go wrong by doing what's right for the kids. At the very least, you'll sleep better.

YOU CAN'T GO WRONG BY DOING WHAT'S RIGHT FOR THE KIDS.

I work in a school district with great kids. They are respectful, intelligent, and fun. But every once in a while, one of them messes up really bad. As the superintendent, one of my roles is to hold an expulsion hearing. In my school district of nearly 3,600 students, I average about four expulsion hearings a year. They are rare, and I am sure to point out that fact to students and parents when they appear before me. I tell them that an expulsion is the harshest penalty a school district can administer, which is why it's the superintendent that holds the hearing. I also let them know that 99.9 percent of our students are not recommended for expulsion.

Because I work in a small suburb and expulsion hearings happen so infrequently, the community is almost always aware when a student is subject to an expulsion hearing. As you might imagine, people love to give me their opinions on what sort of punishment I should mete out. Often, those that contact me lean toward vindictiveness and away from mercy. For example, if a student were to make a veiled threat of gun violence on social media, others often lobby that I do not allow the student to return to school for the maximum allowable eighty days.

Of course, each situation is unique, so I weigh the facts carefully, case by case. But most often, a student appearing before me for an expulsion hearing is a good kid who made a bad decision. Notwithstanding the public pressure for me to apply the greatest consequence possible, I try to be as merciful as I can. I put myself in the parents' shoes and imagine what I would want to happen if it were my own child. Expelling a student from school may appease other parents, but is it always the right thing to do? Most often, it is not. Most often, the student needs to be frightened a little, be made to think about how the situation could have turned out worse, and consider how his or her actions have impacted both school and family. Being away from school for eighty days is rarely in a student's best interest. Indeed, school is most often the best place for the student to be.

Years ago, some seniors pulled a prank the week before graduation that left the school facility with some hazardous slippery areas. Some people slipped and fell, but nobody was injured. As you might imagine, I was pressured by many folks to not let the students cross the stage at graduation. To me, there are only a certain number of life events for students. Prom and graduation are among the most important. These are events that not only the students but also their families dream about and spend much time and money planning for. To not let the students participate in commencement exercises struck me as cruel to both the students and their families. I had no intention of causing any more shame to the parents of the kids; they had been embarrassed enough already. When I assigned the students community service and let them walk at graduation, not everyone was happy. But I felt good that I had made the right choice.

When it comes to the more complex decisions—decisions where somebody is going to be mad no matter what you decide—you will always sleep better at night if you make the decision in the student's best interest.

Equal and Fair Aren't the Same Thing

You might think you want to follow the rule book to the letter. After all, when you were a teacher, you respected the administrators who did not waver from the code of conduct. But if all we ever did was follow the rule book, we wouldn't need administrators; we could just pay hourly workers to read the code of conduct and administer discipline accordingly. You are a principal because you have shown the ability to make tough decisions, which often means seeing shades of gray. You may be accused of "not being consistent." That's a euphemism used by critics of your decision-making, people who don't have to make these difficult choices and don't have all the information. The only thing you have to worry about with consistency is to consistently make the best decision for each unique situation.

Look at an issue as simple as attendance. Your school likely has a progressive discipline policy whereby students face certain consequences as they accumulate tardies. The policy makes administration easy. Imagine you have two students who have been tardy to school ten times each. George has been tardy ten times, so he is assigned a Saturday detention. Loretta has been tardy ten times, so she also is assigned a Saturday detention. Easy, right?

But not so fast. George lives in a home where his only responsibility is to go to school. His mother wakes him up every morning, makes him breakfast, and sees that he is out the door in plenty of time to drive to school. But Loretta lives with her grandmother and little brother. Her grandmother has health problems, so Loretta wakes her little brother up, feeds him breakfast, and puts him on the bus. Loretta then drives herself to school, but because of timing, she sometimes gets caught behind a school bus and is late.

Your policy says that both students get a Saturday detention. Sure, the consequence is equal, but it's far from fair. Fairness means looking at every situation independently and making the best decision for each individual student. Again, more important than administrators following the rules is administrators having the wisdom to know when massaging the rules is appropriate.

RULES ARE IMPORTANT. THEY PROVIDE ORDER. BUT EVERY RULE IS ARBITRARY TO SOME DEGREE.

Rules are important. They provide order. But every rule is arbitrary to some degree. If you go to the grocery store and have eleven items, it is okay to go through the express lane of ten items or fewer if nobody else is in line. When you look at each issue independently, though, understand that you will get heat. Plenty of folks demand that everybody follow every rule to the letter simply because they are the rules. But this mindset does not make kids more responsible; it causes them to rebel. Instead, teach and model for students (and staff) that rules are important, but knowing when to adapt them is equally important.

You Don't Help Anyone by Being Dishonestly Kind

You will have to evaluate teachers. You are going to witness activities in classrooms that are—at best—mediocre, and—at worst—harmful. It would be very easy to give a great evaluation to all your teachers to keep them happy. But the right thing to do is confront the problem tactfully and help the teacher improve in the necessary areas. That teacher may be hurt, may be offended, and may even cry or swear. But the second most important job you have (after student safety) is evaluating effectively.

In Ohio we are fortunate to have a robust evaluation system. It has its problems, but overall, it provides a good rubric to help principals lead those conversations with teachers about how they can improve. But whether or not you have a standardized evaluation system or a rubric, it ultimately comes down to having the confidence to tell people news they don't want to hear. Expertise builds confidence, which means learning is a lifelong activity for principals as much as it is for students and teachers. You likely did not get a lot of training in writing evaluations in your graduate program, so you have a responsibility to seek out resources on quality instruction, assessment, and evaluation.

You can start with *Supportive Supervision: Becoming a Teacher of Teachers* by Albert Coppola, Diane Scricca, and Gerard Connors. Also, Richard DuFour, Robert Marzano, Carol Tomlinson, Mike Schmoker, Jay McTighe, and Grant Wiggins are all authors I recommend. Talk to other administrators and get their recommendations. Join a job-alike group where you can have these discussions with other professionals. Whatever you do, you cannot stand still with your knowledge base as you move into the world of administration. As you build your skills, you will develop the confidence to have those hard discussions.

Also, remember that nobody entered the field of education to be average. All teachers at one time had a dream of being the next Mr. Keating from *Dead Poets Society* or Erin Gruwell from *Freedom Writers*. So when you find an area in which a teacher is struggling, have those difficult conversations with a humble attitude. Praise them for the work they do well, and dispassionately discuss their areas for growth. Whatever you do, do not tell teachers they are doing a great job when they are not. The only way you can improve a teacher's performance, thus improving his or her students' academic achievement, is to give truthful feedback.

This struggle is common among new principals and is a struggle I had myself. I had taught only six years before I became a principal, and there I was, responsible for evaluating teachers who had dozens of years of experience. Frankly, I took the path of least resistance early on and gave glowing evaluations to teachers who were not engaging, differentiating, or even teaching the content standards. I had a bit of an epiphany, though, when I evaluated a teacher of English—my area of expertise. The teacher's lesson was boring. It was some lecture about parts of speech, followed by a worksheet on which students would identify them. When the teacher incorrectly identified an adverb as an adjective, my light switched on. I had tolerated boring, but I could not tolerate a teacher who did not even have a mastery of the content.

Let me digress here. You can probably tell from the example that this was a long time ago. As I sit here twenty years later, it shocks me how much time the teachers of my generation wasted on horrible lessons involving boring lectures and worksheets. I was an English teacher, and—outside of my job—never once in my real-world life did I ever need to know if a word was an adjective or an adverb. Furthermore, knowing the part of speech of a word did absolutely nothing to develop my writing skills. These days, I spend a lot of time thinking about how much time we wasted having students memorize this or regurgitate that. Of course, the world of technology was vastly different back then, and students' access to information was much less. But as I sit here writing about the time I observed a teacher improperly teaching adjectives and adverbs, I'm a little embarrassed.

Nonetheless, that lesson was an epiphany for me. I realized that I had an absolute obligation to discuss with this teacher her being wrong on her content knowledge. That content expertise also gave me the confidence to discuss the weakness of the lesson structure. I soon found myself less afraid to tell the truth about a teacher's weaknesses, which also made the praise I offered more genuine. Later in my career, I had exhausted all my efforts with a whole team of middle school teachers who were failing almost 75 percent of their students each grading period. I felt confident in taking the next crucial step of putting these teachers on plans of assistance for their own and their students' sake.

My advice to not be afraid to tell bad news applies to more than your interactions with teachers. You will have to tell parents things they do not want to hear about their children (she was found with drugs, he sexually assaulted someone, she was caught cheating on an exam). You will have to tell community members things they do not want to hear (we will no longer use your photography service because of the poor quality of work). You will have to tell students things they do not want to hear (you were not accepted into the National Honor Society). And you will have to tell your bosses things they do not want to hear (I lost my temper and yelled at a parent).

Treat these difficult times like a Band-Aid. It hurts less when you rip it off fast. When you have to give bad news, delaying the inevitable only worsens your stress level. Give the news, give it honestly, and give it dispassionately. Only then can growth occur.

You Will Never Be Accused of Communicating Too Much

Communicate, communicate, communicate. Keep people in the loop as much as you can about as much as you can, including students, staff, parents, the community, and the superintendent. And while email may be the most efficient, it is also one of the worst forms of communication and suitable only for relaying simple announcements. And never engage in debate via email. Pick up the phone, or make a personal visit. If somebody sends you an email with a question and it takes more than a sentence or two to answer, make a phone call instead. Here are some examples of how our administrative team tries to incorporate as much communication into our work as we can.

We call people back on holidays.

People expect school administrators to return phone calls and emails within twenty-four hours. They don't expect to receive a phone call within five minutes of emailing a concern to an administrator on Easter. But that is exactly what our administrative team does, and it has done wonders for building trust with our parents. In our district, voicemail left on our office phones automatically gets fed to our email. My team knows that phone calls and emails are to be returned as soon as possible, even if that means on a holiday or a weekend. We do not wait twenty-four hours or until the next business day. We call as soon as we have a free minute. We also do everything we can to respond to an email with a phone call.

A few things happen when you return phone calls at unexpected times. First, angry callers are caught off guard. They often choose to leave a message on the weekend, thinking that you will not hear the message until Monday. But when their phone rings three minutes after leaving a message, they have not had time to stew about their anger. When I make weekend phone calls, the person I'm calling often says, "I didn't realize you were working today." And my response is always "I'm not. I'm home with my family. But you have a concern that is bothering you, and I want to help."

Cyber warriors who leave scathing emails are also given a phone call as well. Often, these folks are taken aback by a personal phone call. They would rather engage in an email back-and-forth, where the nuances of tone cannot be sensed. We call these folks back so they can hear the concern in our voices, so we can ask clarifying questions, and so we can diffuse their anger more easily.

I have called people on Easter, on Christmas Eve, and on more Friday nights, Saturdays, and Sundays than I can count. Honestly, it is partly selfish, too. The last thing I want to do is start my Monday with a call to an angry parent. If I can solve the problem over the weekend, we are both happy. And the side benefit is the angry emailer or caller telling his friends and neighbors, "You won't believe who called me Sunday morning." And the trust grows.

We are all on social media.

The very first directive I gave to the Nordonia principals when I became superintendent was for them to become active on Twitter. Twitter is a free social media tool that allows anyone, including school leaders, to share all sorts of information. I had started a Twitter account myself several months earlier when my district was in the midst of its financial struggles. I had been seeing letters to the editor suggesting that the assistant superintendent position was superfluous and should be cut. Being the assistant superintendent and knowing how valuable I was to the school district, I decided to start tweeting to let people know about all the work I did. I used Twitter to show the long hours I was working and the many duties I carried out. Ironically, my plan did not work. When I became superintendent, the board eliminated the assistant superintendent position, and I continue to do the work of both offices to this day.

However, using Twitter had shown me what a valuable tool it was, hence my directive to principals to start an account.

The principals and I use Twitter multiple times daily to relay news about events happening in our buildings, share articles related to education, brag about great teachers and students, and give the community a brief glimpse into our personal lives. We do not tweet about arguments we have with our spouses, of course, but we do want the community to know that we are human beings, we have families, and we are not just stuffed shirts sitting in ivory towers. Twitter makes us real and approachable, and the community loves it.

Twitter has also been a great tool for sharing emergency news, such as calamity days, which is the legal term used in Ohio for closing schools because of disease epidemic, hazardous weather conditions, law enforcement emergencies, inoperability of school buses or other equipment necessary to the school's operation, damage to a school building, or other temporary circumstances due to utility failure rendering the school building unfit for school use. I have called calamity days for extreme cold, a power outage, and even—yes, in Ohio—the aftermath of a hurricane. But, colloquially, we all know these as snow days.

On snow days, I often ask students to tweet me pictures of the books they are reading, and I choose someone at random to win a small prize. Once, I asked students to create YouTube videos showing why they love Nordonia schools. These activities keep me engaged with our students, and parents love seeing the interaction. It has done immeasurable good for our district's image. And, of course, Twitter is free.

My Twitter account (@DrJoeClark) is by and large a professional account. The vast majority of things I tweet and retweet are photos of school events, thoughts about leadership, interactions during education chats, and announcements of snow days. And the community loves it. Parents love seeing pictures of their kids in school.

And residents and alumni love seeing my posts of football updates on Friday nights.

A major benefit to using social media is that it helps build trust with the community. For me, the most powerful aspect of Twitter is showing a glimpse, not of Dr. Clark the superintendent, but of Joe the person. Every so often I tweet something about my kids, or my dog Frankie, or my large family. I might make a comment about a great Cleveland Browns game. I might retweet a funny cat video. While these things might seem innocuous, the community sees me as a real guy with a real family making difficult decisions for a community he loves.

To be clear, certain things should not be shared on Twitter. I would never tweet if my wife and I had an argument. I try to keep political opinions to myself. Retweeted jokes or videos must be appropriate. But having the vulnerability to give strangers a view into my personal life and the willingness to laugh at myself when I mess up (tweeting a photo of the day I wore two different socks or spilled mustard on my tie) makes me somehow more human. Tweeting helped me to break down barriers between the office of the superintendent and the school community, and people soon started to see me as just an average Joe (pun intended) who happens to be the leader of the schools.

As time passed, I began to focus my tweets on student engagement, and continue to do so today. I hold contests in which students can interact with me and win different prizes. They might have to Photoshop me into a winter or autumn scene. Sometimes we do impromptu scavenger hunts. Other times, students might have to post a photo of a school-themed snowman they built, or of themselves reading a book, or of helping their parents around the house.

The prizes vary. Kids love Chipotle, so a ten-dollar gift card for a burrito is a common prize. I have had T-shirts printed up with my regular snow-day prompt to READ A BOOK, PLAY OUTSIDE, AND

HELP YOUR PARENTS AROUND THE HOUSE. Or maybe it is a mystery box of fun, full of stuff I have collected at trade shows.

The contests are to engage students, but a side effect is parents and community members seeing that I have a sense of fun, that I enjoy students. These interactions become the talk of parent-teacher association (PTA) meetings and, I imagine, family parties. And they build trust. You trust people you like, and who doesn't like a guy giving out free T-shirts and telling students to help their parents clean the basement?

If you do not have a Twitter account, or even if you already do, I recommend you follow these tips:

- Create a username that is easy to find.
- Use a profile photo; don't be an egg.
- Tweet positive stuff only; don't complain or disparage.
- Follow lots of people. The way to get followers is to be a follower.
- Engage in education chats. You will learn a lot and make great connections. And it's okay to simply lurk the first few times.
- Avoid trolls. Public arguments are never a good look for an educator.
- Keep it mostly professional, but give glimpses into your personal life.
- Keep it appropriate—no off-color jokes, drinking of alcohol, and so on.
- Do not follow students.
- Have fun! Be creative with different games to engage staff, students, and parents.
- People love pictures. Include pictures with as many tweets as possible.

In addition to helping me earn the community's trust, Twitter has been great for me professionally. My professional learning network (PLN) includes world-traveling people who speak at conferences and to school districts around the globe. George Couros, Beth Houf, Tara Martin, Jimmy Casas, Marisol Rerucha, Todd Whitaker, Dave and Shelley Burgess . . . these and so many more Twitter users are way up in the stratosphere in making the most of the tool. But even average Joes like me—nondescript guys from Northeast Ohio—can find real value in using Twitter.

In fact, all superintendents and principals should be on Twitter now. If you do not have experience with Twitter, my advice is to start small. Try to post one tweet a day, and keep it positive. Follow some of the great education leaders who are on Twitter, engage in some chats, and soon you will see your followers grow and the tool become increasingly valuable to you and your district.

Several other social media tools exist for you to share information with parents and community. Twitter is my application of choice, and one that I use as myself, but my district also has a Facebook page. Some schools use Instagram or YouTube or any of a variety of other applications. Whichever social media tools you use, make sure you actually use them. It is better to not have a Twitter account at all than to have an account and never post. When you set up an account to engage in social media, you are making the commitment to keep active and to share both good and bad news. If you announce to your community that you are using a social media tool, parents and community members expect to see regular content.

We have a great key communicators program that encourages community investment in our schools.

I started this program upon becoming a superintendent. Jamie Vollmer's book *Schools Cannot Do It Alone* provides a prescriptive approach to engaging the community in meaningful dialogue about the changes we need to make in education. I modified the structure of Vollmer's framework to create a way to rebuild communication, transparency, and trust in Nordonia schools.

The district administrators and I brainstormed a list of more than 130 recognized leaders in our community. These leaders were elected officials, presidents of PTAs and booster clubs, leaders of community organizations, ministers, and so forth. They represented civic clubs, churches, municipalities, homeowners' associations, and more. I mailed a personal invitation to each of these folks, inviting them to become one of my key communicators. I then followed up with emails and phone calls.

I asked the key communicators for two things. First, the leaders allowed me to add them to an email list through which I send timely information about the district. This method of communication maintains transparency and gives our community leaders facts about the school district directly from me. As leaders of community organizations, they meet with community members often. My sending timely information to the key communicators enables them to clarify rumors that their constituents might hear. Almost every bit of information I send to the key communicators is then placed on our district website. Anytime something happens in the district that I think will be a topic of conversation in the community or make the news, I share the facts with my key communicators. This information of interest has included the sale of land, an electrical fire on a bus, a student bringing a toy gun to school, and more. I share the facts with the key communicators, and they share the facts with their constituents, keeping the majority of the community in the loop.

Second, the key communicators each invited me to a meeting of their group, not for me to talk but to listen. I called these my "three-questions meetings." As the name implies, I went to each group to ask three simple questions: What do you like about Nordonia schools? How can the schools improve? What do you expect of your new superintendent? I held many meetings, and it took a lot of time. But I used the data collected from my three-questions meetings to help build our new five-year strategic plan, and I am confident our plan focuses on issues that are important to the community. My key communicator program has been an overwhelming success, and all it cost me was a few stamps to start the program.

We maximize our use of local media outlets.

Many school districts have small local newspapers that are understaffed and begging for news. Nordonia is no different. Upon becoming superintendent, I asked the editor of our local paper, *The News Leader*, if I could write a monthly column. He was more than happy to oblige. Indeed, we were doing each other a favor. The simple purpose of the column is to provide information about various school programs and legislation that affects our schools.

If you have a small local newspaper, reach out to see if you can get some space. We know from survey data in Nordonia that most people in our community, 80 percent of whom do not have kids in the schools, get their information from the paper. It is a wonderful tool, and what does it cost? Nothing.

We are also very fortunate in Nordonia to have a local cable channel, Community Focus.

Each month, I record a twenty-eight-minute show called *Network Nordonia*, to which I invite a guest or two to discuss various aspects of our school district. Guests have included principals, teachers, counselors, central office administrators, and students. We talk about changes related to the curriculum and special education. We discuss the upcoming sports season. We talk to parents about how to discuss drugs with kids. And the highlight show every year is our "Senior Showcase," in which five graduating seniors talk about their positive experiences with the schools.

If you have a local cable channel in your area, contact it to see if you can create a show. If there is no local cable channel, record your own show and upload it onto your district website. It is another way for you to reach your community. And it is free.

Not communicating is not an option. As the district's educational leader, I must ensure that the entire community engages in the educational process. Community engagement is more than parents attending open houses and fans coming to football games on Friday nights. Having true community engagement means leading the discussion about the purpose of education and the vision the community has for its schools.

Not having a public relations person on staff or not having money for glamorous newsletters is no excuse. There are many ways for you to communicate with your public for free. Get on Twitter. Start a key communicator group. Write a newspaper column. Create a TV show. All these tools will increase your visibility, transparency, and trust with your community. And they won't cost you a cent.

When Someone Asks You to Take a Pie in the Face or Kiss a Pig or Sit on a Roof, Say Yes

You did not become a principal to be bored sitting behind your desk. Have fun. It's the best job in the world. When you are given an opportunity to make a great story, say yes. For example, once I ran a quarter mile dressed up like a hot dog. To the general public, that statement might seem incredibly bizarre. If you are a school administrator, you shouldn't even give it a second thought.

When you become a school leader, you know that you will have to deal with curriculum and instruction, teacher evaluations, student discipline, and phone calls from concerned parents and community members. What you might not expect is that you also have to do some crazy things for the sake of the kids.

One of our elementary schools was holding a race to raise money to build an outdoor learning lab. I was dressed as a hot dog, a PTA dad was dressed like a chicken, and a Title I tutor was dressed as a box of Wheaties. We ran a lap with the principal to show the first and second graders where they were supposed to go. The fundraiser made about $24,000, and the outdoor learning lab will be an awesome addition to the school grounds.

In my career, I have been dunked in a tank, had a pie smashed in my face, dressed in a Shrek costume, refereed a powder-puff football game, and played Santa Claus. I know of other school administrators who have kissed a pig, ridden a donkey, skydived, slept on a roof, been taped to a wall, and so much more. They don't teach you about those things in grad classes. But the truth is it's a whole lot of fun, and acting goofy with kids is one of the best parts of the job.

Never Punish a Crowd for the Sins of One or Punish a Child for the Sins of a Parent

If you are an assistant principal, chances are a major part of your job will be student discipline. Discipline can be messy. It takes hard work, investigating, and tough decision-making. Reflect on what discipline means. The word *discipline* comes from the word *disciple*, meaning "follower." Discipline is not something we do to kids; it's something we want kids to have. If you get a thrill doling out punishment, you are in the wrong profession. Administrators in charge of discipline must have a growth mindset and an attitude of mercy. The goal is to give the least severe consequence that will produce the greatest amount of behavior change. We do not yell at students when they can't read; nor should we yell at them when they can't behave properly. Administrators must look at every discipline situation as an opportunity to teach children to be better people.

Don't take the easy way out by punishing a group of kids for the actions of one. Sometimes this happens when a substitute teacher leaves a note saying the class misbehaved while the regular teacher was away. The temptation is to give the whole class a detention or perhaps take their recess from them. While you are likely punishing the perpetrators, you are also punishing a lot of innocent kids. It's just not fair, and no adult would stand for it.

Imagine driving down a highway when you come upon a police roadblock. Officers are approaching each car as it stops to give each driver a speeding ticket. "But I wasn't speeding," you say. And the officer replies, "Well, a lot of you were speeding, and I can't tell which of you were, so I am giving everybody a ticket."

Do not subject kids to such treatment. Sometimes that means somebody breaks a rule and gets away with it. So be it. That's better than being unfair or unjust. When you are unfair to students, it doesn't teach them to follow rules; it teaches them to hate school.

When I worked as an assistant superintendent, a high school assistant principal called me to say that a teacher reported a theft of some money from her desk. The teacher knew it had happened during a certain period, and the assistant principal called me to ask if she could search every kid in the class. That was a big no. Probably the most important class you took in getting your principal credentials was school law. You need to know what a legal search is, and you also need to have a huge level of common sense. A few years back, a principal lost her job because she checked to see what type of underwear students were wearing to the high school dance. Common sense should tell any administrator that was a bad idea.

When a rules violation is reported to you, you need to take the time to conduct a thorough investigation. That means talking to witnesses and the accused, and you have to play by the rules. You need reasonable suspicion to search a student. The search must be limited in scope and reasonable at its inception. If a student is accused of having a gun, you can't search his phone or his lip balm case, as it is not reasonable that you would find a gun in either. Sometimes your gut tells you a student violated a rule. Unfortunately, a gut feeling is not enough to issue consequences.

Last, do not punish a student for the sins of the parent. It's not a second grader's fault for being tardy to school every day, so don't give the student detention for breaking the rule. Treat your students with dignity and respect, and they will treat you in kind. Kids will make mistakes. Be merciful. Don't tell kids not to cry over spilled milk and then yell at them when they spill it. Don't hold grudges. Instead, use kids' mistakes as an opportunity to teach them how they could have acted. Teach by example, administer consequences dispassionately, and always allow a kid a second chance.

New principals and school leaders, you are about to embark on the greatest job in the world. When I became a principal, I spent most of the summer before I started the job worrying about things like budgets and boilers. I was worried that I would not know how to complete state-mandated reports and would have no clue what to do if a bathroom flooded. What I have come to learn, though, is that success for a principal is not defined by exceptional reports and dry floors. Successful principals are those who hold relationships dear to their heart, who treat kids well, who communicate clearly and often, who have the confidence to give bad news, and who have the wisdom to guide those in need. Great principals see their jobs as a calling, an opportunity to serve others for the sake of children.

EVERY DAY THAT YOU GO TO WORK, YOU HAVE THE ABILITY TO POSITIVELY IMPACT A CHILD.

If you are a new principal, it's because somebody saw those qualities in you. Every day that you go to work, you have the ability to positively impact a child. Embrace this opportunity with humility. You have what it takes to do great things. Good luck, and get out there and do them.

You Are a School Administrator BINGO

B	I	N	G	O
Kissed a pig	Had date night with spouse at school event	Ate lunch standing up	Spent a week's salary on student fundraisers	Worked a polling place
Consoled a crying parent in office	Mandated by superinten-dent to attend community event	Admonished misbehaving kids (not your own) at mall or restaurant	Was only staff member to attend PTA meeting	Had your head shaved
Have had spouse accuse you of speaking to him/her like a student	Spent the night on the school roof	FREE	Been held up in grocery store by parents for longer than an hour	Consoled crying teacher in office
Apologized for someone else's mistake	Played donkey basketball	Been asked work-related questions on personal Facebook	Been told you were taking pay freeze	Have eaten disgust-ing-looking food given as a gift so as to not hurt a stu-dent's feelings
Arrived at work and left work in the dark on same day	Spent a week's salary on clothes, food, and/ or supplies for needy students	Consoled crying student in office	Took a pie to the face	Worked a spaghetti dinner or pancake breakfast

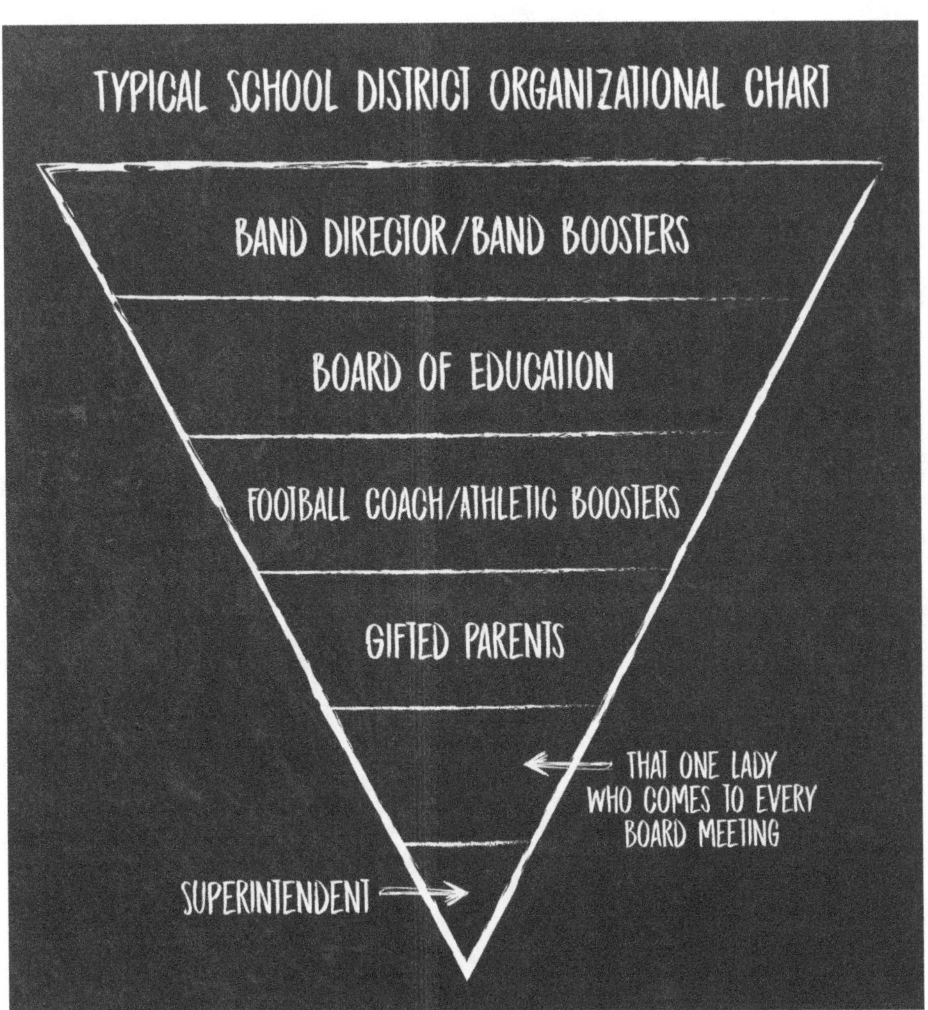
TYPICAL SCHOOL DISTRICT ORGANIZATIONAL CHART
BAND DIRECTOR/BAND BOOSTERS
BOARD OF EDUCATION
FOOTBALL COACH/ATHLETIC BOOSTERS
GIFTED PARENTS
THAT ONE LADY WHO COMES TO EVERY BOARD MEETING
SUPERINTENDENT

—2—

SCHOOL LEADERSHIP IS MORE THAN SNOW DAYS

It's not just snow days. School leadership, I mean.

The vast majority of a school leader's angry calls and emails and tweets come on days with blistering cold and accumulating snow, days when you try to gather as much information as you possibly can and make a decision in the best interest of student and staff safety. Days when you are up at 4:30 a.m., texting your colleagues, calling your maintenance staff and city road crews and police departments. Days when your car is the only one in the parking lot and you answer the door for parents who—for whatever reason—didn't get the message that school is closed. Days when the value the community places on your ability to lead the schools is based on your reading a weather forecast and making a decision that might just as well have been a coin flip.

And you are grateful for the people who email you on days like that and tell you that they don't envy your job and can sympathize with how tough it must be to be a school leader on a day like this. And you get irritated by those who email and tell you what a fool you are.

But you want the truth? Snow days are among the easiest problems we deal with.

School leadership is much more than snow days.

School leadership was the week when we worked with a family whose daughter was fighting an eating disorder.

School leadership was the week when we worked with a family battling alcoholism.

School leadership was the week when we worked with a family who could not afford to pay their school fees because the father was laid off from his job.

School leadership was the month when we worked with a family whose mother went to prison and the children had no place to stay.

School leadership is when staff members lose parents and spouses and children to disease and accidents and suicide.

School leadership is when daily decisions made for the betterment of the community are attacked by fringe residents with personal agendas.

School leadership is encouraging staff to work with the kids who nobody wants to work with, the disadvantaged and disruptive and challenging, because school leaders know that kids' futures are better with the skills we help them gain in the thirteen years they are with us.

SCHOOL LEADERSHIP IS SERVICE TO OTHERS. PERIOD.

And making decisions about snow days? Comparatively, that's easy.

If we can agree that leadership is service, the question then becomes, What does that really mean? What specific skills must one have to live a life of service as a school leader? The list is endless, of course, but it includes showing compassion and giving care to those marginalized in your community, mediating conflict, remembering and tending to the most vulnerable, and modeling for staff how to also tend to them. Below are some examples of situations in which I found myself exploring how to serve my school system and community in just those ways.

Caring for the Vulnerable

Unfortunately, sometimes tragedy gives you an opportunity to serve.

In the spring of 2018, toward the end of one day, I got a phone call from the middle school principal saying a student had just been hit by a car close to the front of his building. I jumped in my car and headed toward the scene. I got about halfway there and found myself stuck in traffic. The ambulance had arrived, and traffic was stopped. I was still a few hundred yards away from where the ambulance was, where a handful of students had gathered. So I parked my car on the shoulder of the road and sprinted there.

Upon reaching the scene, I saw that the ambulance had just left to transport the student to the hospital. The middle school principal was there, and he let me know it was a high school student who had been struck. The boy had met his brother at the middle school and was walking with him to a local store when he crossed in front of traffic and was hit.

The next thing I thought to do was run back to my car and drive to the hospital, Akron Children's Medical Center, one of the most renowned children's hospitals in the nation. On the way, I called the high school principal, Casey Wright, who met me there. We walked into the emergency room and met the attendant at the information desk. We shared that one of our students had been hit by a car and that we were his school principal and superintendent. The attendant was flabbergasted.

"Wow," he said. "I've never seen a principal or superintendent come to visit a student before."

Casey and I laughed out loud.

"You're kidding," Casey said. "We do this all the time."

And he was not exaggerating. When we have a student in the hospital, we visit. It is not to show the parents our commitment, or even to show the kids our support. It is because we care about our students like they are our own children, and it is the right thing to do. That doing so builds relationships and trust with the parents, who then tell their friends and neighbors that we were there, is a pleasant consequence.

Earlier that same school year, one of our student-athletes suffered a stroke during a Saturday cross-country meet. He was transported to University Hospitals' main campus in downtown Cleveland, and Casey and I went to visit him together the following Monday. Again, the amazement of the hospital staff to see school administrators there visiting a student was telling. We felt bad that we had not gotten there sooner, but the parents were overjoyed to see us, and we spent some time joking with the student that I would grant him a snow day when he got better.

This student had a miraculous recovery. He was unable to walk when we first visited, and his speech was greatly slurred. But by springtime, he was running in a school track meet again. Later he was honored as the University Hospitals' Comeback Athlete of the Year, which, of course, we attended.

Another time, Casey spent the night at the hospital after a soccer game in which a player experienced a severe injury, causing him to be life-flighted to care while his parents were out of the state. And nearly every other time we learn of a student in the hospital, we make sure an administrator visits. Sadly, we have attended more than our share of funerals, too, for students and their family members. It is the right thing to do.

Learning to Take Criticism

My parents were married on June 25, 1955. On March 25, 1956—nine months to the day after my parents' wedding—my brother Dave was born. In 1957 came my sister Karen; 1958, Perry; 1959, Chris; and 1961, Kim. Then my parents slowed down for a while and had only six more of us over the next ten years. I was last, born in 1970, the youngest of eleven. Seven boys and four girls.

Dave, Karen, Perry, Chris, Kim, Patty, Steve, Kelly, Mike, Paul, Joe.

My mother is a saint.

My siblings will tell you that being the youngest of eleven caused me to get all sorts of extra attention and spoils. My siblings lie.

Having ten older siblings, particularly six older brothers, put me in harm's way most of the time. There's the time my brothers pinned me to the kitchen table and shoved lime Jell-O down my pants because they said I had taken too much. There's the time my brother Dave was watching me for the evening and made me scrub our shower with my toothbrush for some sin I can't recall. Dave also smacked me on the head with a sledgehammer one time, but that was accidental, a sort of Three Stooges "when-I-nod-my-head-you-hit-it" type of buffoonery.

But my brothers also prepared me for my career more than any graduate-level educational leadership course ever could. You see, when I was a kid, my brothers used to make me climb to the top of our wild cherry tree, and then they would throw baseballs at me. Nothing has prepared me for my career in educational leadership quite as much.

Leaders in all professions are thrust to the top of their organizations, sometimes by choice, sometimes by chance. In education in particular, those leaders then find themselves the target of attack after attack after attack. Being a superintendent is not much different. By its nature, the job requires me to make choices. And when choices are made, someone is always angry their wishes were not met. It could be something as simple as calling (or not calling) a snow day and as serious as deciding to allow a student to walk at graduation after pulling a dangerous senior prank.

The baseballs come flying.

"The weather is terrible! Why are we in school?" WHACK!

"You're letting the kid who poured baby oil on the cafeteria floor walk the stage?" WHACK!

"What do you mean you are upholding the suspension?" WHACK!

"You are only offering a two percent raise? We deserve four percent!" WHACK!

"Quit asking for a levy! Do more with less!" WHACK!

Often, I think of the timid Albert from the inappropriate but hilarious movie *A Million Ways to Die in the West.* When Anna pushes Albert to stand up for himself against the town's scourge, Albert says he is no hero. In fact, he says, "I'm the guy in the crowd making fun of the hero's shirt."

Climbing to the top of the tree is a courageous act. It's lonely, and the baseballs come whizzing by. People who would never have the guts to take on a leadership position feel all too comfortable telling you about all the mistakes you've made. So I thank my brothers for thickening my skin, for letting me experience the pressure of the attack, for preparing me for the job I love so much.

How can I love it? Because despite the baseballs being fired at me, the view from the top of the tree is incredible. I get to see kids who have struggled with any number of issues cross the graduation stage. I get to approve leave for staff members who are struggling with illness. I get to hire excited teachers ready to come into the district and change kids' lives for the better.

The view from the top of the tree far outweighs the baseballs that whack me in the head every so often. If you are a school leader, I hope your view is as nice as mine. And if you are a teacher fearful of ever becoming a school leader, don't give it a second thought. Yes, the baseballs can hurt. Just rub some dirt on the sore spots and get back out there.

Mediating Conflict

When I was an assistant principal, I would describe my job this way: I go to work, wait for someone to mess up, and then wait to get yelled at for it. If a student misbehaved in class, say, and I ended up assigning a Saturday detention, I got it from all angles. The student and his parents were mad because the punishment was too severe; the teacher was mad because the punishment wasn't harsh enough; a board member was mad because the misbehaving student was his neighbor's kid; and the principal was mad because his office was dragged into the mess. It didn't matter that I had no control over the interaction between the student and the teacher that caused the problem in the first place. As judge and jury, I was the one who would invariably take the heat.

I have grown professionally over the years, I believe, in my ability to mediate conflicts. A hugely helpful resource is the all-time classic book by Dale Carnegie, *How to Win Friends and Influence People*. I have come to find that the theme is applicable to every leadership position. Our job descriptions as leaders necessarily give us the responsibility to make difficult decisions. And as we all know, every decision has people on both sides who will disagree.

Do you remember the old Trident gum commercials that said, "Four out of five dentists recommend sugarless gum for their patients who chew gum"? Even dentists couldn't agree on what kind of gum their patients should chew.

Interestingly, the most stressful part of my job—making difficult decisions—is the most liberating. As a leader, I have the ultimate authority to make decisions that I believe are fair and just. It's not fun getting heated emails or phone calls or reading about yourself in letters to the editor. But when I put my head on the pillow at night, I sleep well knowing I did the right thing.

A leader must have a set of core values on which decisions are based. Your conscience, not your critics, should determine your course of action. So my message to anybody in a leadership position now or aspiring to be a leader is this: you will never escape criticism, so just do what's right.

YOU WILL NEVER ESCAPE CRITICISM, SO JUST DO WHAT'S RIGHT.

However, I understand saying "just do what's right" is pretty nebulous. Who determines what is right? As a leader, you have an integral role in determining right from wrong, and doing so is easier if you stop to consider your core values. A set of core values is like an anchor: when the stress of a decision and the lobbying from multiple parties for different outcomes make you feel like you are being tossed about on an angry sea, core values calm the storm.

In my district, our administrative team adheres to these core values, developed throughout the years as we considered challenges, decisions, mistakes, and successes:

- Treat students like they are our own children.
- Build strong relationships with parents and community.
- Admit and correct our mistakes.
- Do all things with honesty, integrity, and ethics.
- Commit to the mission of service to others.

When we are faced with a tough decision or being challenged or bullied to make a certain decision, we look at our core values and determine our course of action. The best course of action is always the high road.

The Importance of Taking the High Road

"Joe, remember you have no friends."

A superintendent I worked for told me those words many years ago as we discussed my hopes become a superintendent one day myself. What she meant was this: when you are superintendent, you are by yourself. You have no comparable person in the school district. You have nobody you can go to for advice or venting. You are on your own. As Alan from the film *The Hangover* might say, "You are a one-man wolf pack."

Every month or so, I get together with a group of superintendent colleagues from the area. We discuss current topics in the field, weigh in on difficult issues we are working on to gain different perspectives, and learn from each other about how to better serve our communities. During one of these meetings, one of the most meaningful pieces of advice came from a colleague across the county: "The best path from point A to point B is the high road."

Leaders in any field are subject to a continual barrage of criticism. The same is true for superintendents, principals, teacher leaders, board members, PTA presidents—anybody in a position of leadership. People use a variety of methods to criticize the decisions you make and the policies you enact. They even make personal attacks. The critics sometimes appear at public meetings. Sometimes they write anonymous letters. Sometimes they send emails or write letters to editors, or even take out paid advertising.

Their hope is to draw you into an argument or a debate to put you on the defensive so that you appear unprofessional or imbalanced. While it can be tempting to engage in arguments, the best path from point A to point B is the high road. The greatest leaders rise above their critics. They do not stoop to the level of personal attacks or get drawn into unwinnable debates. School leaders need to remember that the high road is the only road to take. Even when critics attack and bully and try to pull you into the mud, responding with character is never a bad decision.

Earlier I wrote about one of the toughest moments of my career, when I was ordered to appear before the Ohio Elections Commission on charges that I had violated state campaign law. The fact is I violated the law, I realized I did, I corrected my mistake, and I apologized for it. Nonetheless, the PAC that had reported me to the state elections board wasn't satisfied with the ruling of no punishment even if I had made proactive steps to correct my mistake.

Almost monthly, one of the PAC members would write a letter to the editor of our local paper and come to our public school board meetings, where they would profess to all that I was unfit to lead and that I was a bad example to our district's children. These constant attacks were hurtful and embarrassing. Also, they were goading me to react angrily so they would have more ammunition about my unfitness to share with the public. It was incredibly difficult, but I took the high road. I chose not to engage in the debate, and I did not retaliate. Eventually, many community supporters came to my defense at a board meeting where they criticized the PAC members for being so vindictive. Despite my admitted mistake, my standing in the community improved. People respected me for keeping my composure in the face of the public attacks.

In one district where I worked we offered a tuition-based, full-day kindergarten program. In Ohio, half-day kindergarten is required for all public schools. However, school districts are permitted to charge parents for full-day programs as long as a sliding tuition scale is offered. Children who qualify for free or reduced lunches are required to pay only a portion of the tuition. I remember sitting in one administrator meeting discussing the program, and somebody recommended not publicizing on the kindergarten flyer that kids living in poverty could get reduced tuition. The person argued that we could raise more money if people were not aware of a discounted rate.

I was appalled that someone on our administrative team would have the audacity to recommend something so heartless, and I was even more disgusted when the rest of the team actually spent much of the meeting considering the recommendation. The high road was calling for me to leave that district, and my time there was unsurprisingly very short.

Sometimes situations arise when a student may be a candidate for a leadership position or a scholarship and one or both of the student's parents play an active role in the school district. Perhaps they are an employee, a PTA officer, or an active booster. The temptation is to consider the parents when making decisions about their student. But never give in to that temptation. Taking the high road means practicing genuine impartiality. It also sometimes means showing mercy to a student. For example, if a troubled child is up for expulsion, the high road is considering what is best for that child, not listening to the demands from parents of "the good kids" who want the student kicked out of school.

The Importance of Not Giving In to Threats

Taking the high road refers to making decisions and acting in ways that are morally and ethically sound. But sometimes school leaders are simply subjected to bullying by somebody who wants something and uses real or perceived power to influence a decision.

It happens more often than you would think.

From time to time, parents or community members or sometimes even staff are fixed on something they want or need, and they will attempt to get it through implicit or explicit threats, not through reasonable discussion. Maybe they want something for their child: a changed grade, more playing time, transportation privileges, or a detention cancelled. They may want something for themselves: a new assignment, a granted leave, a waived fee, or access to unavailable facilities.

The threats may be covert. Statements like "I've always supported your levy" imply that next time they might not. Emailed complaints cc'd to a board member or supervisor imply that I will be in trouble if I don't do what they want.

The threats may be overt. Sometimes they threaten litigation. Sometimes they threaten to never support a future levy if their wishes aren't granted. Almost always they remind you that they are taxpayers and pay your salary.

Here's the thing they don't think about: they don't want a school leader who gives in to threats. Why not? Because if a school leader gives in to their threat, isn't that leader just as likely to give in to a threat from somebody else?

And, quite frankly, sometimes people ask for exact opposite outcomes. For example, it's not uncommon when students have a conflict at school that one parent will demand that the other student be suspended, while the other parent will demand their child not be disciplined at all, with both parents threatening never to support the school again if they don't get what they want.

So people really do not want school leaders who cave in to threats. Instead, they want school leaders who listen to concerns, who consider all sides of the issues carefully, and who make the best decision they can based on the best information they have gathered.

Sometimes decisions must be black-and-white. But most often, good school leaders are expected to have the ability to make reasonable decisions in more complex situations. Clearly, not every decision will make every interested party happy. But when you think about it, wouldn't you really rather have leaders who sometimes disagree with you than ones who concede every time they are threatened with adverse consequences?

Accepting Bloody Knuckles with Grace

I'm not a bird watcher. I don't have binoculars. And I have never taken part in a Big Year, a competition in which birders compete to identify as many different species as they can in a year. But I do like birds. I have two double shepherd's hooks in my backyard, and I like to relax on my deck watching the birds eat at the feeders that hang from them.

Not long ago, I noticed that a sparrow at my feeder had gotten itself stuck. Its foot was pinned at the point where the two hooks come together. The bird was hanging there helplessly, and I decided to free it. As I reached toward it, the sparrow started flapping his wings and pecking at my hand. I grabbed it and let it go, then looked to see my hand covered in scratches.

Unbelievable. Here I was trying to free this helpless little bird, and the only thanks I got were some bloody knuckles. But that's life, right? How many times do you try to free a bird, only to find yourself with a pecked hand? It happens all the time with our kids: eat your vegetables; get to bed; brush your teeth; put the video games away; do your homework. These are all things that are good for the kids, yet we're often thanked with rolled eyes, outright obstinacy, or the passive-aggressive "whatever."

We do it, too. My doctor always tells me to avoid sweets, and I know that avoiding sweets is in my best interest. But if there's a chocolate chip cookie within a hundred yards, I will sense it and seek it out. My doctor tells me what I should do for my own good, and yet I totally disregard his advice. He's trying to free me from the shepherd's hook, and I am fighting him all the way.

School leaders—all leaders, really—periodically free birds, only to have their knuckles bloodied. One of the toughest jobs a leader has is delivering bad news to people. Often, that news is in the best interest of the receiver to hear, but it might be returned with anger, threats, letters to editors, and slanderous behind-the-back comments. This backlash can happen when a school leader is referring a student for an IEP against the parents' will, making personnel decisions, altering bus routes, redistricting school buildings, or recommending controversial policy changes—all tough decisions, all carefully considered, and all what is believed to be in the best interest of the student or parent or staff member or district.

And yet we know that with every decision, somebody will be unhappy. And we know, too, that not deciding *is* making a decision. So what's the answer? Ultimately, leaders need to be guided by our conscience. Even though we may be criticized or attacked, we need to do that which is virtuous and good and fair and honest. You will get bloody knuckles in your career as a school leader. It is inevitable. The secret is learning how to cope when that happens. It's really easy to say, "Don't take it personally." But the problem with that statement is that I am a person, and you are a person, so we are going to take it personally.

One must-have for school leaders is your own small professional learning community, or PLC, of maybe one or two other people. In this PLC, you do not need to talk about curriculum and new legislation and the substitute teacher shortage. Instead, make it a PLC for venting. You need one or two people who you trust and who you can be totally vulnerable and honest with, people who you can cuss and be unprofessional with. It helps if you choose others who have the same job you have (but who aren't in your school district), so they have a deeper understanding of the circumstances you face. The relationship must be embedded in trust, so you can let off steam without worrying that your words will come back to haunt you. Whatever you do, do not take your frustrations out on your significant other or your dog.

Of course, healthy eating and exercise do wonders to relieve stress. I am the best- and worst-case example of this. I have lost forty pounds, gained it back, then lost seventy pounds and gained it back. When I was at a reasonable weight, I ran five half-marathons and many 5Ks. And when I am not at a reasonable weight, I still like to get outside whenever I can and walk in the woods. You do not need to be a marathoner. Just get outside into nature and take some time for yourself.

Let's also remember that seeking counseling is not a sign of weakness. Trained counselors provide confidential space for you to work through your issues, and often their services are covered by your medical plan or your Employee Assistance Plan. Even counselors themselves commonly seek counseling—they consider it standard operating procedure to get support for doing their own weighty jobs. Let's be honest. School administration is also a tough job, and counseling is a great way to deal with work-related stress.

Cannot-Dos and Must-Dos of Being a Superintendent

CANNOT-DOS	MUST-DOS
Give the finger to bad drivers.	Buy fundraiser crap from every student who asks.
Yell at referees.	Pretend to root for local college and professional sports teams.
Get the morning paper in your underwear.	Appear proud of teachers nominated for "Who's Who Among American Teachers."
Express any sort of political opinion.	Appear to be interested in many boring stories.
Win 50/50 raffles or prize baskets at school fundraisers.	Appear sympathetic to teachers who have to work evening open houses or conferences.
Appear to be happy about calling a snow day.	Pretend to enjoy a baked good gifted to you by students.

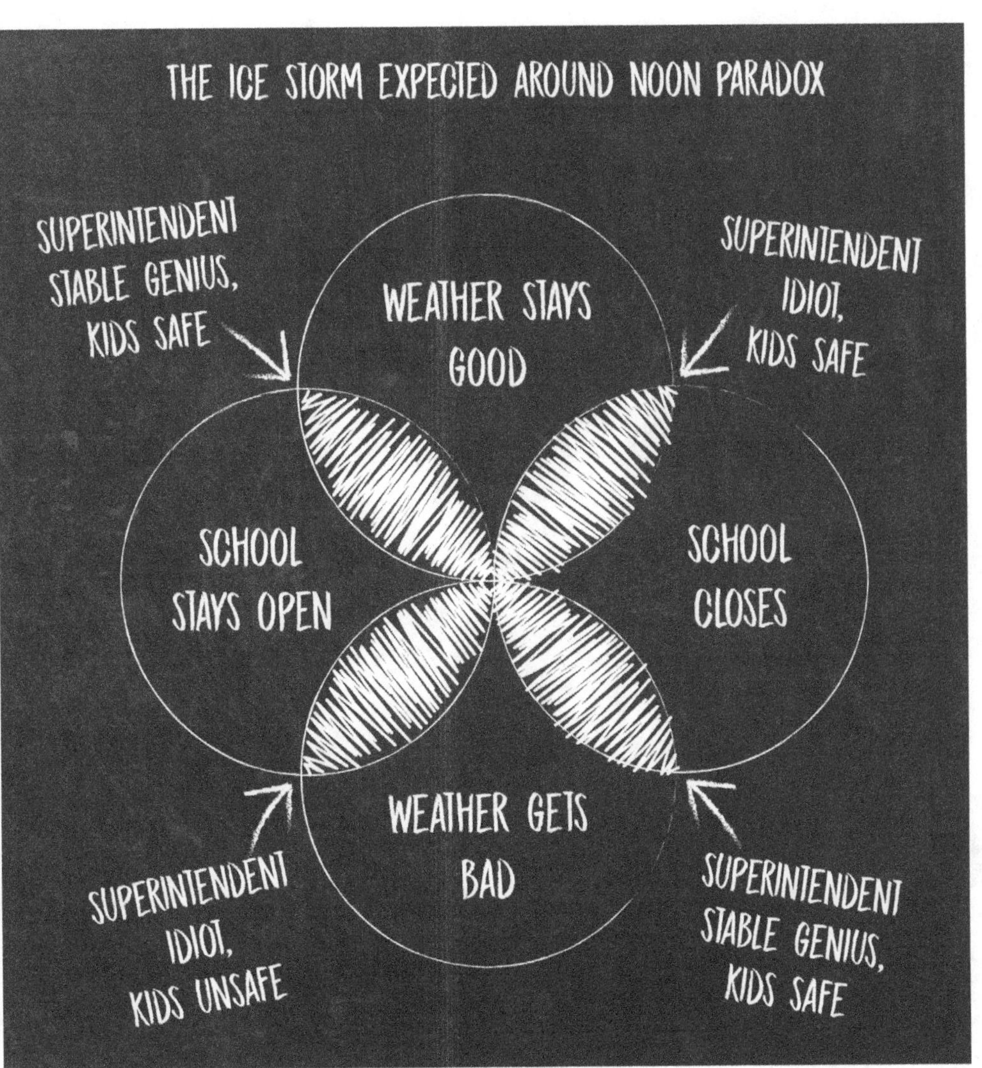
THE ICE STORM EXPECTED AROUND NOON PARADOX
SUPERINTENDENT STABLE GENIUS, KIDS SAFE
WEATHER STAYS GOOD
SUPERINTENDENT IDIOT, KIDS SAFE
SCHOOL STAYS OPEN
SCHOOL CLOSES
WEATHER GETS BAD
SUPERINTENDENT IDIOT, KIDS UNSAFE
SUPERINTENDENT STABLE GENIUS, KIDS SAFE

—3—

MAKE EVERY DAY OPENING DAY

Opening Day of Major League Baseball. It's like a baptism, when the sins of yesteryear are washed away. Hope is in the air. Anything is possible. The World Series is there for any team to take, for any team who finds some good pitching and some timely hitting and a little bit of luck. On Opening Day, even the Chicago Cubs are contenders.

Opening Day. We forget about all those pains from the past. We forget about Jose Mesa in Game 7 of the '97 World Series. We forget about Steve Bartman, the Cubs fan who interfered with a foul ball that would have been caught for an out, leading to what Cubs fans believe to be the failure of the team to win the pennant in 2003. We forget about Bill Buckner, the Boston Red Sox first baseman who watched a ground ball pass between his legs, leading to what Boston fans believe was the cause of the Red Sox's losing the 1986 World Series. Opening Day is the ultimate do-over. We all start fresh. We are all 0-0 with 162 to play.

Opening Day is also a part of spring. I'm not a huge fan of spring myself—too much wind, too much mud, and even if the sun is out, it is often too sloppy to get any good yard work done. But I also understand the symbolism of spring: rebirth and renewal. It's when ugly gray days are replaced with sunshine and color. Each of us has that opportunity to create a spring for ourselves. If there is something we are not happy with, spring reminds us that we can change, that we can grow.

In the school business, we constantly encourage students to change and grow. But the truth is, adults can learn a lot from kids. Often, the changes we need most to make are in ourselves. Indeed, ourselves are the only thing each of us can really change.

So as we get ready for the crack of the bat and the roar of the crowd in the stadium, let us educators also remember that for our students, every day should be Opening Day.

Every day should be a chance for kids to start fresh.

Every day should be a chance for kids to turn the corner; to take a new path; to grow; to change; to continue developing into the creative, intelligent, caring, compassionate adults they are all capable of becoming.

Opening Day is about mercy and forgiveness.

Opening Day is about second chances.

Opening Day is about realizing that the role of the educator is not to condemn for past failures but to help up, to brush off, and to set forth on the straight path.

Kids are kids. They make mistakes. They make bad choices. They cause others pain. They strike out, sometimes a lot. But they are still kids, still capable of rebirth and growth, still deserving of another opportunity to come to the plate. And if we continue to coach them, they will hit it out of the park.

How awesome would it be if every day were Opening Day for our students? If every day, every student everywhere was given the opportunity to start fresh? Educators have the power to make that happen. Make the choice to do so.

One way to make that happen is to dissuade and disallow conversations among staff members that often happen at the beginning of the school year or as next year's class lists are being prepared. Those conversations typically start like this: "Oh, I see you have Johnny on your roster . . . good luck!" or "Hey, what can you tell me about Louise? Didn't she get suspended for fighting last year?" Of course, there is certain information related to a student's health issues or disabilities that must be shared among teachers. But as a principal, you need to do all you can to squelch any talk that paints students in a bad light even before the year begins.

It is also important to reaffirm with your staff that when students do get in trouble, we are disappointed in the behavior, not the child. Furthermore, once the discipline is served, the child has a clean slate. I repeat that: kids do make mistakes. We all do. But just because a student breaks a rule and gets in trouble, even a significant rule, does not mean we should treat that student like a bad person. Kids will meet whatever expectations we set, and if we expect students to misbehave because of their past, we are setting them up for failure in the future.

The consequences we administer must be both immediate and reasonable for the level of the infraction. Principals should avoid following blanket policies that prevent participation in major school events far into the future. For example, I witnessed a situation where a student involved in a fight in December (after being bullied for being homosexual, to make it worse) was told he would not be able to go on the class trip to Washington, DC, in May. I angered some teachers when I allowed the student to go on the trip, but I met with them to share my reasoning behind the decision. Such policies are made solely for the convenience of adults who feel their chaperoning duties will be easier if they refuse any kid who may cause any sort of trouble. But these policies are entirely unfair to the student, and they are counterproductive. If the rationale for the policy is to make sure kids behave all year, doesn't it stand to reason that a student banned from the trip in December has no incentive to behave through the rest of the year?

I have seen similar situations in which students were denied the chance to go to prom or to walk the graduation stage. To be clear, there are certain times when banning is a perfectly reasonable consequence, depending on the severity and frequency of a student's misbehavior and the proximity to the event from which the student is being banned. But, in general, we need to remember that discipline is what we want kids to have, and it is our responsibility to help them get it. Being excessively punitive and holding grudges damage relationships and kill a good school culture. Let's remember the joy of Opening Day, of starting anew, and remember to be merciful to kids so they can have the fresh start they deserve.

I've experienced firsthand the importance of first days and new beginnings. I was absent from my first day of kindergarten. I don't remember much about it other than it was 1975, I was four years old, and I stood out front by my mailbox for what seemed like hours, waiting for a bus that never came. Over the next thirty-seven years, I did not miss another first day of school as a student, a teacher, a principal, or a superintendent.

My streak ended on August 22, 2013. While four thousand Nordonia students began what was another incredible year, I was in Syracuse, New York, dropping off my oldest son, Isaac, at college. (Go, Orange!) I knew I was going to be sad. I kept catching myself tearing up when speaking to people about his leaving. But I couldn't be more excited for the opportunities that lay before him. His life was a blank canvas, and on that day in August, he opened the first jar of paint.

As a career educator, to me, this is what it is all about. And those four thousand Nordonia kids who come through our doors each year? I want for them exactly what I wanted for my own son. I want them to be curious, to be risk-takers, to be prepared, and to be committed to making the world a better place. I want them all to experience the first day of college or be prepared for fascinating careers in jobs that may not even exist yet. I want them to know that they can do and be anything they want. My job—no, my mission—is to ensure that we provide them with the skills and self-confidence to follow their dreams. After all, this is the most important new beginning in their lives, and it's what we've spent thirteen years preparing them for.

I have always thought one of the best parts of my job is that every year I get a new start. For people in other professions—law or medicine or policing or accounting—time runs together. Seasons come and go, but there is nothing like the cycle of the school year that marks our profession. In the world of education, every year we come to an end and then have a break to reflect on what we did well and how we can do better. We relax a bit and then start fresh in the fall with a new group of students. I love this sense of renewal, and we owe it to our students to provide them, too, with a sense of renewal, not just every autumn but every time they fall. We know kids are going to make mistakes. When they do, we must be quick to help them move on and start fresh. We can't warn others about the bad

WE OWE IT TO OUR STUDENTS TO PROVIDE THEM, TOO, WITH A SENSE OF RENEWAL, NOT JUST EVERY AUTUMN BUT EVERY TIME THEY FALL.

kids coming, and we can't hold grudges against students for crimes they've paid the price for. Ultimately, our mission is to prepare students to enter the world of adulthood. But while they are kids, let's focus on mercy instead of retribution.

Interscholastic Sports Weather Calendar

July

Su	Mo	Tu	We	Th	Fr	Sa
1	2	3	4	5	6	7
8	9	10	11	12	13	14
15	16	17	18	19	20	21
22	23	24	25	26	27	28
29	30	31				

August

Su	Mo	Tu	We	Th	Fr	Sa
			1	2	3	4
5	6	7	8	9	10	11
12	13	14	15	16	17	18
19	20	21	22	23	24	25
26	27	28	29	30	31	

September

Su	Mo	Tu	We	Th	Fr	Sa
						1
2	3	4	5	6	7	8
9	10	11	12	13	14	15
16	17	18	19	20	21	22
23	24	25	26	27	28	29
30						

October

Su	Mo	Tu	We	Th	Fr	Sa
	1	2	3	4	5	6
7	8	9	10	11	12	13
14	15	16	17	18	19	20
21	22	23	24	25	26	27
28	29	30	31			

November

Su	Mo	Tu	We	Th	Fr	Sa
				1	2	3
4	5	6	7	8	9	10
11	12	13	14	15	16	17
18	19	20	21	22	23	24
25	26	27	28	29	30	

December

Su	Mo	Tu	We	Th	Fr	Sa
						1
2	3	4	5	6	7	8
9	10	11	12	13	14	15
16	17	18	19	20	21	22
23	24	25	26	27	28	29
30	31					

January

Su	Mo	Tu	We	Th	Fr	Sa
		1	2	3	4	5
6	7	8	9	10	11	12
13	14	15	16	17	18	19
20	21	22	23	24	25	26
27	28	29	30	31		

February

Su	Mo	Tu	We	Th	Fr	Sa
					1	2
3	4	5	6	7	8	9
10	11	12	13	14	15	16
17	18	19	20	21	22	23
24	25	26	27	28		

March

Su	Mo	Tu	We	Th	Fr	Sa
					1	2
3	4	5	6	7	8	9
10	11	12	13	14	15	16
17	18	19	20	21	22	23
24	25	26	27	28	29	30
31						

April

Su	Mo	Tu	We	Th	Fr	Sa
	1	2	3	4	5	6
7	8	9	10	11	12	13
14	15	16	17	18	19	20
21	22	23	24	25	26	27
28	29	30				

May

Su	Mo	Tu	We	Th	Fr	Sa
			1	2	3	4
5	6	7	8	9	10	11
12	13	14	15	16	17	18
19	20	21	22	23	24	25
26	27	28	29	30	31	

June

Su	Mo	Tu	We	Th	Fr	Sa
						1
2	3	4	5	6	7	8
9	10	11	12	13	14	15
16	17	18	19	20	21	22
23	24	25	26	27	28	29
30						

Rainy season   Spring sports season

—4—

IT'S EASY FOR YOU. YOU'RE CREATIVE: BOARDS OF EDUCATION AND THE 5-0 VOTE

I've heard of a school district in which a handful of concerned citizens gather monthly to watch school board meetings on local cable access. Allegedly, these folks play a game in which they take a drink every time the board of education votes 5-0. Ignore the disturbing fact that these adults are playing a drinking game—not exactly the type of role modeling you'd want from adults in your community. Instead, focus on the cynical arrogance of these folks, likely the same folks who would criticize a board as being disjointed if they were to have a split vote.

I have been attending school board meetings in three different school districts for the past twenty years or so. I can probably count on two hands the number of votes that were not 5-0. Does that mean that boards of education are simply rubber stamps for the superintendent? Hardly.

Most items that boards of education vote on are things that are nothing more than legal requirements or routines. For example, boards of education must vote to accept donations. They vote on accepting minutes from previous meetings. They vote to renew contracts for insurance and natural gas and electricity. They vote to go into executive session. They vote to adjourn. It is not surprising that these votes are almost always unanimous.

Boards of education also vote on many personnel matters: accepting resignations, hiring staff, renewing contracts, and so on. Recommending personnel matters to the board is the primary responsibility of the superintendent and is what a superintendent spends the majority of time doing. Even if an individual board member does not fully agree with any one individual personnel decision, the board understands that it hired the superintendent to make those decisions. After all, the superintendent does all the background work—not the board—and the board generally trusts the superintendent, a trained professional school leader, to make good decisions.

So a board of education is not left with much more to vote on. These remaining matters might concern initiating a contract with a particular vendor, asking the community for a levy, or selling and buying property. In these cases, a 5-0 vote still does not symbolize a rubber-stamp board. Indeed, 5-0 votes in these matters are evidence of a strong relationship between the board and the administrative team.

Dave Burgess, before he entered the writing, publishing, and speaking field full-time, was a brilliant teacher in San Diego (you should follow Dave on Twitter @burgessdave). Dave talks about how six of the worst words a teacher can say to a colleague who has engaging lessons are these: "That's easy for you. You're creative."

Why is that insulting? For two reasons. First, it minimizes all the teacher's hard work in creating an engaging classroom. That result doesn't just happen. It happens because somebody took the time to know the students; planned activities, questions, procedures, and assessments that were appropriate for those students; and then delivered outstanding lessons. Second, it takes the teacher who speaks those words off the hook. If teachers believe that achieving excellence is some sort of innate ability, then they will believe there is no point in working hard because they will never be as engaging a teacher anyway.

So make the correlation to a 5-0 board vote. The person who says a board that votes 5-0 is just a rubber stamp for a superintendent minimizes all the hard work and compromise the board and administrative team accomplished in work sessions and discussions, sometimes for months leading up to a vote. These discussions are difficult and involve a lot of growth and a lot of compromise. The 5-0 vote symbolizes what is great about the system. The arrogant cynic, comfortable at home playing his drinking game, just doesn't get it.

Moving on from the critics, though, how can school leaders help achieve this kind of consensus? You won't be surprised when I say communication. Except for maybe birthday parties, nobody likes surprises. This is especially true with boards of education and superintendents. Boards of education do not want to vote on something they know nothing about, and superintendents do not want to be blindsided in a public meeting with questions they have not prepared for. To prevent those instances, there must be communication, communication, and more communication.

Even for noncontroversial items on an agenda (e.g., accepting donations and approving minutes), I give my board of education a month's notice of the coming recommendations. We use a web-based agenda generator, and board members have access to the agenda literally the second I start producing it. They know it is in draft form, and they can see every item as I add it to the agenda. I start the document for the next month's board meeting the day after the current month's board meeting, so there is always something for the board to review. Before we started using the web-based system, I would have a preboard meeting to go over the agenda with the board president and vice president. The web-based system is an improvement because all the board members can see the agenda developing in real time.

For controversial items (e.g., changing the level of transportation service we provide), items that will expend a lot of district funds (e.g., changing our insurance carrier), and new or revised board policies, I begin discussions with the board at least two months in advance. Every Friday, I send my board a formal weekly update, in which I inform them of issues in the district and upcoming recommendations. If there are emergency issues (e.g., a bus accident or student injury), I do not wait until Friday. I provide those reports as they happen. The bigger the issue, the more time I allow for the process. Even as I write this, I am working to develop an incentive-based pay system for our administrators. I have told the board I will not ask them to vote on the issue until May at the earliest (it is currently November), giving us seven months of discussion in work sessions before I am ready to make a recommendation.

Throughout this whole period, board members are free to ask me questions, and I can answer them. However, it would be a violation of sunshine laws for the board to engage in discussions outside of a board meeting, such as via email. That restriction makes it vital that I allow plenty of time for us to have public meetings for hashing things out. It takes a great deal of time and hard work, but usually the result is a unanimous vote because we have taken the time and made the effort to come to consensus. And most often, if someone is going to vote no on an item, we know before it happens, and we know the reason why. No surprises, but certainly no rubber stamps.

I am a die-hard Browns fan. Every Monday morning, I have a hundred ideas about how the Browns could have done better the day before. But the truth is, no matter how much smarter I think I am than the Browns coaching staff, I'm not. It's easy to be a Monday-morning quarterback. But until you are actually in the game, it is probably best to reserve judgment.

PART 2

CAMP IS FOR CAMPERS

A Student-Centered Approach

—5—

CAMP IS FOR THE CAMPERS (AND SCHOOL IS FOR THE STUDENTS)

I am a huge proponent of summer camp. Kids need to spend their summers outside getting dirty, swimming, telling ghost stories, singing silly songs, making cool crafts, playing games, and making friends.

I suppose I'm biased. For ten summers, from my high school graduation until I became a principal, I worked at CYO Camp Christopher in Bath, Ohio. I started as a bus driver and counselor and eventually became the day camp director for six seasons. Some of my greatest memories, some of my greatest friends, some of the greatest life lessons I've learned, all came from Camp Christopher. I met Amie at camp and asked her to marry me on the shores of beautiful Lake Marian.

When I was the day camp director, I often found myself saying something that eventually became the staff's motto: "Camp is for the campers." For example, if I saw a counselor dipping into the tater tots as we were setting up for lunch, I'd say, "Camp is for the campers," and the counselor would know not to eat until after the kids had all been served. If counselors were sitting at a table socializing when they were supposed to be in the field playing wonderball or Indian ball or counselor hunt or whatever else with the kids, they'd hear, "Camp is for the campers."

Eventually the entire counseling staff embraced the motto and used it to keep their fellow counselors in check. A camper telling a joke and the counselor spoils the punch line? "Camp is for the campers." Not feeling like getting dirty on Bury Your Counselor in the Sand Day? "Camp is for the campers." Not feeling like doing the motions to the "Alligator Song"? "Camp is for the campers." Not wanting to participate in Day Camp Jug Band or Counselor Beauty Pageant or Peanut Butter Bird Feeders? "Camp is for the campers."

Camp *is* for the campers.

And similarly, school is for the students.

THIS LITERALLY IS A LIFE-OR-DEATH PROFESSION.

Education is a tough job. Standards are getting tougher, evaluations more severe, pressure higher, funding cut, criticism tougher. But school is for the students. And whenever the adult world of school weighs on us, we need to remember that we are here for the kids. We have to persevere, we have to build positive relationships, and we have to create engaging lessons because our kids are counting on us. This literally is a life-or-death profession. We are the only chance some students will ever have to break free from a life of poverty. As the field of education continues to go through massive overhauls, one thing will never change: school is for the students.

Big Joe, Camp Mom

I will always remember my first day as a camp counselor. Camp Christopher Day Camp ran a bus that picked up campers at area churches each morning. The bus almost always started at St. Vincent (directly across the street from St. Vincent-St. Mary High School, alma mater of one LeBron James). The bus would then take a different route each week, picking up at parishes in different parts of the county. If we were going to West Akron, for instance, our route would be St. Vincent to St. Sebastian to St. Hilary to camp. If we were going to the northern part of the county, it might be Holy Family to St. Mary to St. Barnabas to camp. And so on. We counselors were each assigned a different church, where we would meet the campers, collect their outstanding paperwork and payments, and ride the bus with the kids to camp.

On my first day, I was assigned to St. Sebastian, and I was quickly introduced to a seven-year-old girl named Brynn. Brynn had never been to camp, and she was crying. The bus arrived, and we hopped on. I sat with Brynn, who continued to cry.

"What's wrong?" I asked. "Are you nervous about camp?"

Through tears, Brynn sputtered, "I . . . I . . . I . . . miss . . . miss . . . my . . . mom."

The crying went on for the duration of the trip. When more kids boarded at St. Hilary someone asked Brynn why she was crying, and her answer was the same: "I . . . I . . . I . . . miss . . . miss . . . my . . . mom."

We always sang songs on the bus from the time we left the last church until the time we arrived at camp. Brynn cried throughout song time, despite the humorous lyrics declaring, "There is a booger in my sugar (no, it's not)," "Sam Sam the lavatory man was scooping up the poopies in his little tin can," and "We are CYO born and CYO bred, and when we die we'll be CYO dead, dead, dead, dead."

(Yes, camp sing-alongs are disgusting and gruesome, and more kids need to partake in the whimsical genre of camp songs.)

We arrived at Camp Christopher and went into the Monday routine, starting with counselors getting the list of their campers. I was assigned the seven-year-olds, and as I called out their names, I recognized one: Brynn, the girl who missed her mom and would not stop crying. I discussed the rules with my group, we came up with a group name, and then we headed out for the typical Monday morning activity: a long hike through the camp's 164 wooded acres. As we hiked, I stopped often to tell stories of Mummy's Cave, which contained the mummified remains of Fanny, a woman pushed (allegedly) down Fanny's Hill after an argument with her husband in Old Man's Cabin, where she found him beating her cats against the chimney, which was the only part of the cabin remaining after the horrible fire caused by some curious Boy Scout trespassers who were held captive by the Old Man and tried to cut their ropes using the broken glass of oil lanterns.

(Yes, camp stories are violent and imaginative, and more kids need to partake in the whimsical genre of camp literature.)

So we took a long hike and finally worked our way back to the day camp area in time for lunch, when I noticed something. Brynn, who was holding my hand, was no longer crying.

"Brynn," I said. "You're not crying! Don't you miss your mom anymore?"

Brynn said, "Big Joe, you made me forget that I had a mom."

I was eighteen years old at the time, just having finished my freshman year of college. If I had been ambivalent about my plans to be a teacher, Brynn confirmed my calling in life for me that day.

So many Brynns come to our schools every day. Some miss their moms. Some don't have moms. Some have to play the mom for younger siblings. Some come from homes of abuse or neglect or drug use. Some are hungry, some tired, some dirty. Some are homeless, some are anxious. Some have suffered any variety and any number of traumas in their lives.

For many, the best part of their day is going to school, where they are cared for, fed, loved. Yes, sometimes we feel pressure to increase test scores and raise student achievement. But never, never forget your responsibility—privilege, really—to first be a mom to your students.

Be caring. Be nurturing. Be available.

Just don't sing any songs about boogers.

Candy Is Delicious Food. Eat Some Every Day.

Many things changed between the start and end of my career as a camp counselor. Frankly, as time went by, things seemed to get less gross and more safe. In my early years—the late 1980s and early 1990s—we sang songs about boogers, we rode horses without helmets, we tried to get the kids to get as loud as they could on the bus rides to and from camp, we drank bug juice all day, and using sunscreen was unheard of.

By the time I left the world of camp, things had softened. Booger songs were set aside for "The Song That Never Ends," helmets were mandatory at the stables, we were silent on the bus when we were crossing a railroad track, campers had to drink a cup of water with their lunch before they were allowed a cup of bug juice, and slathering kids with sunscreen became part of the morning routine.

One other significant change was snack. By the late 1990s, the afternoon snack we provided campers consisted of things like yogurt, fresh fruit, and graham crackers. But back in the day, sugar was king.

Lemonheads.

Jolly Joes.

Gobstoppers.

Atomic FireBalls.

It was candy, and it was delicious. And just in case you forgot how delicious it was, inside each package a reminder was printed in bold letters: CANDY IS DELICIOUS FOOD. EAT SOME EVERY DAY.

That slogan became the camp staff's mantra. It was our reminder to embrace the joy in life, even those days when joy was hard to find. To be honest, finding joy at camp was never really a hard thing to do. But if a thunderstorm caused us to cancel swimming for the day, candy was still delicious food.

It may be harder to find joy in a classroom. Work is work, and the most engaging lessons, the lessons that students absolutely love doing, can still be difficult and stressful. Add in the workload of your students' other classes and the unknown stressors the students face at home, and even the best teachers may struggle to keep things light from time to time. If your lessons are not engaging or you're being mean or unreasonable, that makes things even worse.

But candy is delicious food. Look for ways to give your students some every day. That candy may come in the form of a smile, a sticker on a paper, a three-second stretch break, a happy birthday song sung to a classmate, or soft music playing while students work. It might be telling a story about your dog or calling for a take-your-shoes-off day. It might even be actual candy (but avoid nuts and have some sugar- and dye-free candy on hand for students with those restrictions).

Some of you are reading this thinking, "This is ridiculous. Kids don't need candy every day. We need to prepare them to be adults." But, I ask you, don't you love when the waiter brings your bill and includes some mints with it? Don't you love buying a soda or a snack from a vending machine and finding an extra quarter in the change slot? Don't you love when you go to the hardware store, and it's free popcorn day? Don't you love when someone asks if you lost weight? Or notices your haircut? Or comments on how cute your bag is?

Can't any of those things turn a bad or average day into a better one?

Candy is delicious food. And you have the opportunity to satisfy the sweet tooth of each of your students—every day.

Check the Hill before You Slide

The scene: the warm afternoon of a long, rainy day at Camp Christopher. Weather-related cancellations of swimming and horseback riding. About 120 kids stuck in a pavilion all day, singing, hearing stories, and making craft-stick projects. Counselors as stir-crazy as the campers. So—finally—we decided it was time to break out the Slip 'N Slide.

For those of you who do not know what a Slip 'N Slide is, you missed out on one of the great joys of childhood. A Slip 'N Slide is a sixteen-feet-long sheet of yellow plastic with a sprinkler system running the length of it. When you attach a running hose to the sprinkler system, water wets the plastic, which is fastened to the ground with metal spikes. On flat ground, kids get a running start, dive onto the Slip 'N Slide, and enjoy a wet ride. Sometimes a kid might get cut by one of the spikes, but mostly it is a safe, fun activity.

When you put your Slip 'N Slide on a hill, however, it can become a deathtrap.

Adjacent to the day camp field was a grassy hill, maybe fifty feet long, leading to the ranger's house. On this particularly wet day at camp, we decided to set up the Slip 'N Slide at the top of the hill. Kids could get a running start from the ranger's backyard and hit the Slip 'N Slide at a pretty good speed. With the help of the sprinkler system and the falling rain, it was not long before kids started sliding further than the sixteen feet of plastic. The littlest kids, our five-year-olds, were going maybe a foot or two beyond the plastic. The biggest campers, the twelve-year-olds, were going a good ten feet past the end of the plastic, aided by what had become a mudslide.

We were having a blast watching the kids cruising down the hill, and then I said something stupid. "Hey, Yoko," I said. "I dare you to go." The real Yokozuna was a 589-pound professional wrestler during the heyday of the World Wrestling Federation. The camp counselor Yoko earned his nickname because he was, at that time, a larger fellow (though today he has shed a lot of weight and is an avid runner).

After I dared Yoko to ride the Slip 'N Slide, the campers caught on and started chanting his name.

"Yo-ko! Yo-ko! Yo-ko! Yo-ko!"

Yoko was all in. We cleared the landing area of campers, and he backed up to get a running start. He hit the plastic like Clark Griswold riding his saucer sled. It was an explosion of mass and velocity, and when Yoko reached the end of the Slip 'N Slide, he kept going.

And going.

And going.

Spinning like a windmill, Yoko continued down the hill, his girth keeping him on a path in the direction of a large metal pole, upon which sat a majestic birdhouse filled with starlings. Yoko's momentum dropped to zero as he hit the pole with his midriff, wrapping around it like a taffy pull.

The kids erupted in cheers, and it was only after the cheering stopped that we heard the painful groans of Yoko. One of the campers yelled, "Get him out of the way!" And the sliding continued.

Instantly, I regretted the pressure I had put on Yoko, and the pressure I had allowed other staff and campers to put on him. Fortunately, Yoko was okay. He might have bruised some ribs, but nothing was broken. Today we are able to laugh about that story, especially about the kid yelling at us to pull him out of the landing zone. But it is also one of those moments I look back on even today as a leadership failure on my part.

I am not minimizing my role in setting Yoko up. It was the challenge from me that spurred him on to ride the slide. The lesson here is peer pressure is not just felt by kids. People in leadership positions are pressured by the crowd to act all the time. It might be parents pressuring a superintendent to call a snow day. It might be teachers pressuring a principal to suspend a disruptive student. It might be a union pressuring a board to give a raise it can't afford. It might be a teacher being pressured by colleagues to go along with a departmental practice they know is wrong. Or it might be kids chanting for you to ride a Slip 'N Slide.

But when you do ride, and you wrap yourself around a birdhouse pole, the kids aren't the ones who feel the pain of bruised ribs. They just yell for you to get out of the way. When you are sliding through mud and it is too late to stop, you will be the one who ends up hurt.

If you are a school leader, and you feel pressured by a person or a group to make a decision, take the time to look down the hill and see what it is you might be crashing into. People love telling leaders what to do because they know they won't be held responsible for the leaders' actions. Check the hill before you slide. Take your time, look at the landscape, and make the best decision because it is the right decision, not because others are chanting your name.

If You Can't Find a Turtle, Be the Turtle

Recently I was reminded of a story from my days as a camp director.

We had themes for each week of the summer, and we programmed activities around each theme. For Western Week, we always had a "gold rush," during which we would paint small rocks gold and hide them around the camp for the campers to find.

During Music Week, we had the Day Camp Jug Band. All of us counselors would bring some kind of instrument from home, whether we could play or not, and put on a concert for the campers.

I could give a thousand more examples, but you get the point.

So during Animal Week each year, each group of campers was supposed to catch a turtle sometime during the week. On Friday, the groups painted their turtles and we would have the Great Camp Christopher Turtle Race Championships. (Don't worry. We used water-soluble paint and released the turtles afterward.) One year, counselor Mike's group couldn't find a turtle. (Mike is in the picture below, furthest left in the second row, standing in front of a much-younger me.)

After searching and searching and searching for a turtle all week without success, Mike came up with a great solution: *he* would be the turtle. Mike let his campers paint his back, and he entered the ring to race the real turtles. And recently, fifteen years later, a camper remembered it fondly enough to remind me of it on Facebook. What is Mike doing today? Of course, he's a teacher.

My time at camp is filled with stories like these, about how we made do with limited resources and used our creativity to make memorable experiences for the campers. During Music Week and our jug band performance, Bianca was the only counselor who could play a real instrument, a saxophone. The rest of us grabbed maracas, sticks, tambourines, and, yes, a milk jug to play a few tunes for the kids. They did not care that we stunk; they just loved being a part of it.

During Time Warp Week, counselor Crazy Joe would grab some towels from the lost and found, wrap himself up to look exotic, and become the Great Mystico, telling the fortunes of our campers. Yoko would portray the GORP monster (short for Gobs of Raisins and Peanuts), a fictional being who came to life as I narrated a story about him terrorizing a little town by stealing all the raisins, peanuts, Froot Loops, pretzel sticks, and whatever other treats the counselors had brought that day. It got really funny when I announced, "Then all of the kids of the town chased the GORP monster across the field and tackled him!" Yoko was a good sport.

If you have not read Dave Burgess's *Teach Like a Pirate*, you need to. In it, Dave talks all about how some creativity can turn a boring class into an awesome class, much like some creativity made Camp Christopher Day Camp such a magical place for thousands of campers over the years.

Camp is for the campers, my friends. And school is for the students. If you are lucky enough to have a job as a camp counselor or a teacher or anything else that allows you to work with kids, make sure you do everything in your power to give them awesome memories that last at least fifteen years.

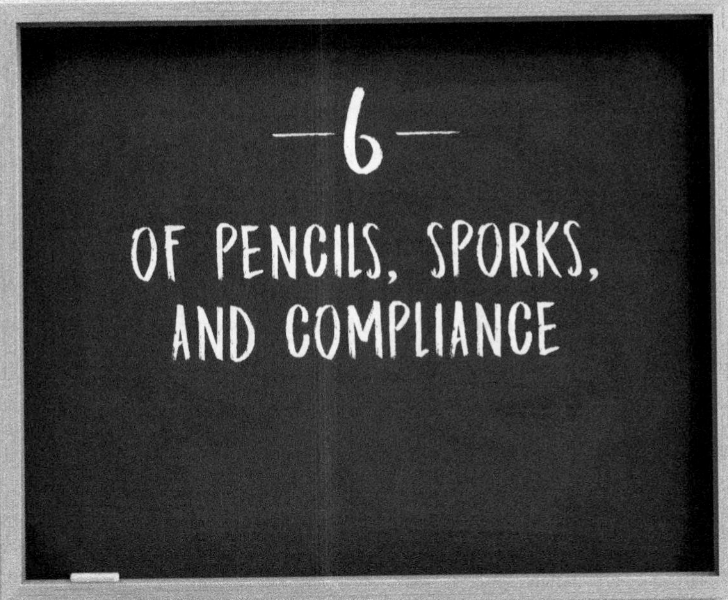

—6— OF PENCILS, SPORKS, AND COMPLIANCE

When I was a middle school principal many years ago, a parent stopped by my office one morning, angry about a grade her son earned on a social studies test. When I looked at the test, it was clear why she was mad. At the top of the test (which was all multiple-choice questions), the teacher had written in black ink: *88% B+.* Great score, right?

Not so fast. With a red pen, the teacher had drawn a thick *X* over the original grade and written next to it: *0% F No Pencil.*

The classroom policy required students to do their work in pencil. (Why? I'm not sure. This was a social studies class, not a math class.) Because the student had taken the test in pen, the teacher gave him a zero on his test. To make matters worse, the student had asked the teacher to borrow a pencil before the test began. The teacher had refused the request.

When I asked the teacher what this was all about, the answer was what you might expect: "We need to teach our students to be responsible." On the contrary, I think she was teaching this student to hate school and to not trust adults.

So what are grades for? Many leading educational scholars argue against assigning grades at all. Many of those arguments have great merit, but I don't want to get into that discussion here. Even if we accept the traditional practice of assigning grades, the question still remains: what is the grade for? It should be a representation of the student's knowledge, right? Not an indication for whether the student used the correct writing utensil. Or headed the paper properly. Or used the proper clear plastic binder. Or any of those other things that measure compliance while we euphemistically say we are teaching responsibility.

I am a grown man with three college degrees. I have a wife and kids and a mortgage. I go to church every Sunday and call my parents on their birthdays. And sometimes I forget my pencil. When I do, I ask to borrow a pencil—or I use a pen—and life goes on. But you might ask, What if doctors were this ill-prepared? I guarantee that if a doctor forgot to bring his scalpel into surgery, he wouldn't use a spork. Somebody would give him a scalpel.

Sometimes I hear teachers say, "But it's part of my job to teach responsibility." That is true. Teach responsibility. Just don't grade it. You want kids to put their names in the upper right-hand corner of the paper to make it easier for you to grade. As much as you might argue that fulfilling your wish is preparing them for the real world, it is not. Sometimes disorganized kids grow up to be disorganized adults, and they get along just fine. So if you want students to follow a procedure, teach the procedure. And if they don't follow it, teach it again. And if they still don't follow it, teach it again. Just like Amie reminding me where my empty soda pop cans go.

In most cases, the procedures we ask kids to follow are for adult convenience. Recognize when this is true, and adjust your expectations accordingly. Does it really matter if a student does his math homework in pen? Does it *really* matter? Does it make him more likely to understand the concepts you are teaching? Of course not. But if you insist it is important because kids need to learn to follow rules, you may need to check yourself. Do you meet every deadline? Do you follow every procedure? Do you never speed, always squeeze the toothpaste from the bottom, and always put the twist tie back on the bread? I don't.

The best teachers I know understand what is most important: making sure kids can understand and apply the content. They have classroom rules, and they expect them to be followed. They don't just freak out when a kid forgets. As you work to teach responsibility, do not lose your temper. Do not yell at kids. Do not get sarcastic with them. And, again, do not grade them on it.

So what happened to the young man and his test? I asked the teacher to change the grade. No, that's not actually right. I didn't ask the teacher to change the grade; I asked the teacher to give the student the grade he had earned. The cries came that I was not supportive of the teacher. But the truth is I was supportive of the teacher; I gave her an opportunity to learn from her mistakes and did so in a way that allowed her to save face with the family.

TO ME, IT'S MORE IMPORTANT TO SUPPORT *WHAT* IS RIGHT RATHER THAN *WHO* IS RIGHT.

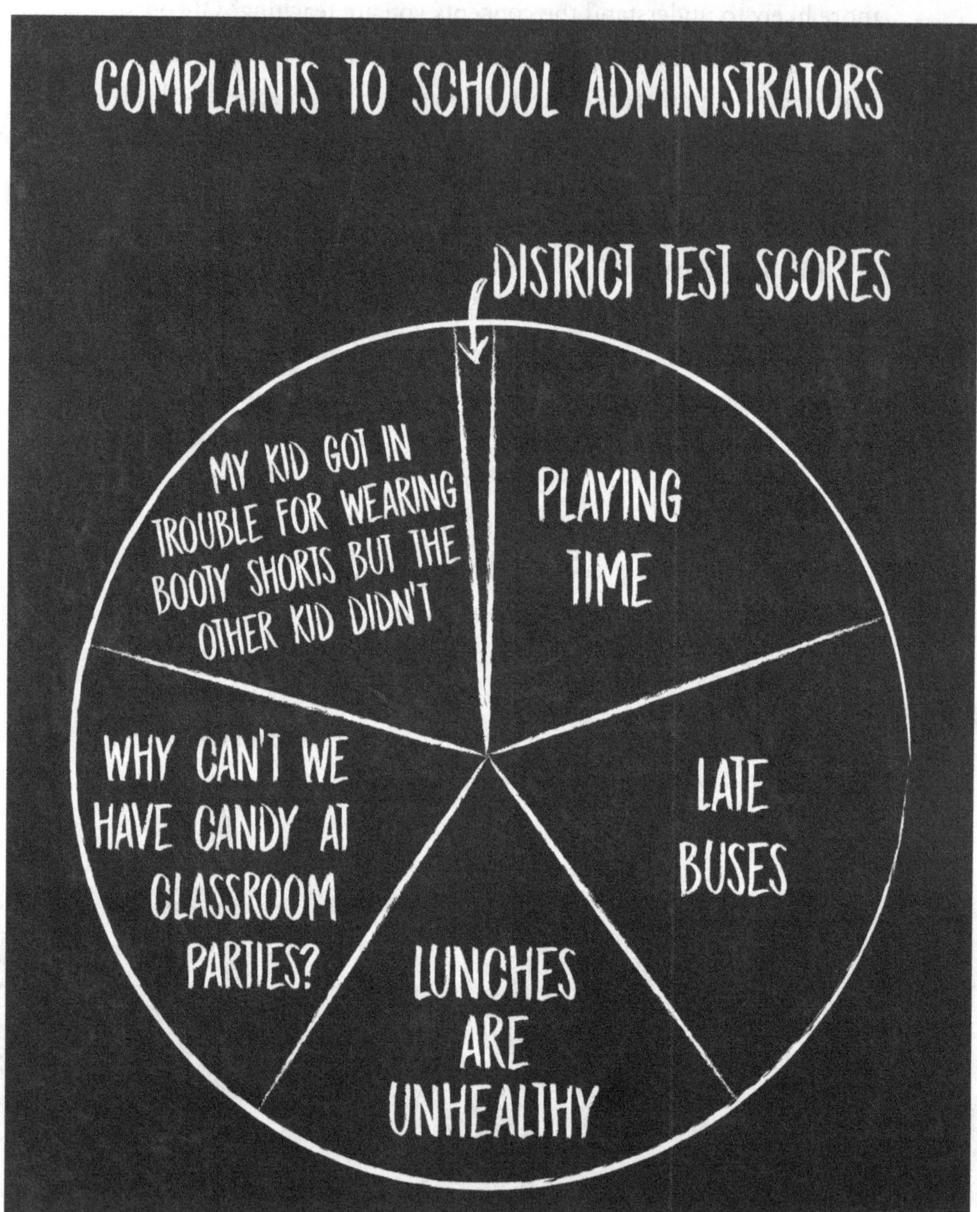
COMPLAINTS TO SCHOOL ADMINISTRATORS
DISTRICT TEST SCORES
MY KID GOT IN TROUBLE FOR WEARING BOOTY SHORTS BUT THE OTHER KID DIDN'T
PLAYING TIME
LATE BUSES
LUNCHES ARE UNHEALTHY
WHY CAN'T WE HAVE CANDY AT CLASSROOM PARTIES?

—7—

BEYOND CONTENT: THE IMPORTANCE OF RELATIONSHIPS IN SCHOOLS

Ultimately, the primary goal of every school is to increase student achievement. But while getting kids to understand and apply content is important, it is not the only thing educators do. Educators teach students how to grow life skills and form relationships. Educators teach students to have empathy and resilience. Educators teach students how to take responsible risks and be good global citizens. Over the years, I have seen all this play out in schools in a number of ways.

Tim is a former student of mine from my days teaching English. I was a classroom teacher from 1992 to 1998, so I had Tim in class many years ago. A few years ago, Tim and I reconnected on Twitter, and one night he reminded me of something that I had long since forgotten.

Apparently, I frequently said, "A clean school is a happy school," and I would get irritated when I saw students drop trash in the hallway and not pick it up. One day between class changes, I put a crumpled-up piece of paper in the middle of the doorway to my classroom. As the kids came strolling into the room, every one of them stepped directly over the piece of trash. Not one of them picked it up.

I then started class with a rather firm discussion about taking pride in your environment, about treating property well, about wanting to go to a school that was neat and tidy rather than one that had trash strewn all over the hallways.

Like I said, I had completely forgotten that I ever did that. But Tim remembered. Even though it was years ago, Tim remembered my lesson.

The lesson was not planned.

The lesson was not assessed on a standardized state test.

The lesson was not one that I even remember giving.

Wow. Sometimes you make an impression on people, and you never even know it. Perhaps you have seen the video about the lollipops from leadership speaker Drew Dudley that illustrates this concept. (If you haven't, the video is available on YouTube. Search "Drew Dudley Lollipop.") Drew tells a simple but profound story. When he was a college student, he randomly gave a new freshman a lollipop during her orientation. What he did not know was that the young lady was scared to death and ready to quit school, but Drew's kindness and humor gave her the courage to continue. Small acts of kindness like that can reverberate in unexpected ways.

I'm not sure Tim remembers anything about *Romeo and Juliet.* I'm not sure he remembers discussing Thoreau's *Life in the Woods.* I'm not sure he remembers what a predicate adjective is. But I am thrilled that he remembered something that still has meaning in his life, and I am honored to know that I made some kind of positive impression on a kid. In Tim's tweet to me, he said he liked my class "BC we learned about life & developed prob solving skills." And he used the hashtag #BeyondContent.

Educators, this is a lesson we can't forget. Content is important, but education is so much more than that. It's about building relationships and teaching life skills that our kids will remember long after they've forgotten what an adverb is. Teachable moments present themselves to us all the time. We need to take advantage of every minute we have with our kids.

Will it change the world? I don't know. But it will make for cleaner hallways.

Every Child Has a Solo

One way that I like to approach the issue of relationships as a school leader is by encouraging teachers and administrators to ask themselves what each child's solo might be. Let me explain what I mean. I realized something when I attended the final choir concert of Isaac's high school career. I won't ever forget that night. Isaac had been performing since fifth grade, and this was the best show of his I had ever seen. And as much as there is to say about the importance of the arts and how music must stay in every school, I want to talk instead about the freshman choir.

The freshman choir performed first that night. They did a medley of songs from *The Lion King*, which was awesome. About twelve kids had solos throughout the performance, and you could easily tell who the soloists were going to be even before they began. You could tell because they were the kids who looked like they had eaten bad fish. They had that "Please don't let me die on stage" look. Sheer terror.

But as each student finished their solo, the audience applauded, and a huge smile engulfed each of their faces. It was like Christmas and a birthday and a snow day wrapped into one. It was pure joy. It was pride in a job well done. It was the exhilaration of knowing they had had the courage to face their fears and come out safe on the other side.

Every child has a solo. That night, the solos were literal, students singing alone on stage in front of a crowd. But whether in the choir or not, every child has a solo. For some, it is on the football field. For some, it's on the track. For some, it's in the art room. For some, it's in math class. For some, it's at church. It's grooming horses. It's painting. It's playing guitar. It's cooking. It's visiting the elderly. It's making friends. It's leading a group. It's writing a poem. It's programming a computer. It's something—anything—where a kid acts on a passion that makes him or her feel successful and at home.

Every child has a solo, a talent, a gift. Every child has something they were put on earth to do. But so many kids spend their days not knowing what their solo is.

It's every adult's responsibility to help them find it.

How? The best way is simply by exposing kids to as many experiences as you can. Be the teacher who fights for field trips, who advises clubs, who starts new clubs based on student interest. Be the teacher who provides choice in assignments, who lets kids use their imagination and design their own assessments. Have lots of books on many topics readily available. Invite guest speakers to your classroom to talk about their vocational or avocational experiences. Listen to and observe your students to find hints for things that might excite them.

My youngest son, Matthew, was not a huge fan of high school. He got good grades, played football, and sang in the show choir. But he didn't really have a passion for anything. That is, until we took him on his first college visit to Bowling Green State University, which happens to have one of the best sports management programs in the country. As Matthew sat through the program's presentation, I could see the spark ignite. When the presentation ended, Matthew turned to me and said, "This is exactly what I want to do."

Matthew ended up going to the University of Louisville (Go, Cards!) and majoring in sports administration. He has worked for two minor league baseball teams: grounds crew for the Akron

RubberDucks and stadium operations for the Louisville Bats. He loves it. It's his passion, all sparked by a college visit.

In my current district, the high school administration recently developed the Student Enrichment Series. The program provides students with high-interest learning opportunities on relevant topics outside of the normal classroom setting during staff professional development days. Since students do not attend school on in-service days, they can instead use this time for self-reflection and personal development.

In its first year, all the workshops were provided at the high school, with topics ranging from leadership development to time management. Led by a combination of Nordonia staff experts and professionals in the field, the workshops allowed students to devote attention to gaining strategies for success that are applicable to every aspect of life.

Now, the program includes exploratory field trips to college campuses, businesses, and health-care facilities. The purpose of the trips is to allow students to investigate fields that build and sustain the future, providing students a window into future careers they may never have considered. For example, a group of students visited HYSON Manufacturing to explore the fields of engineering, chemistry, and manufacturing. Another trip was to Syracuse, New York, for students to explore the environmental science opportunities at SUNY College of Environmental Science and Forestry and to check out the acclaimed Syracuse University College of Engineering and Computer Science. In the future, students will visit the Innovation Learning Lab at Carnegie Mellon University in Pittsburgh.

It's our job to expose students to such opportunities and experiences. To encourage kids to take risks. To pick them up when they are down. To give them a hug or word or kick in the butt at the right time. Every child has a solo. Imagine the choir the world will have when all children have found their part.

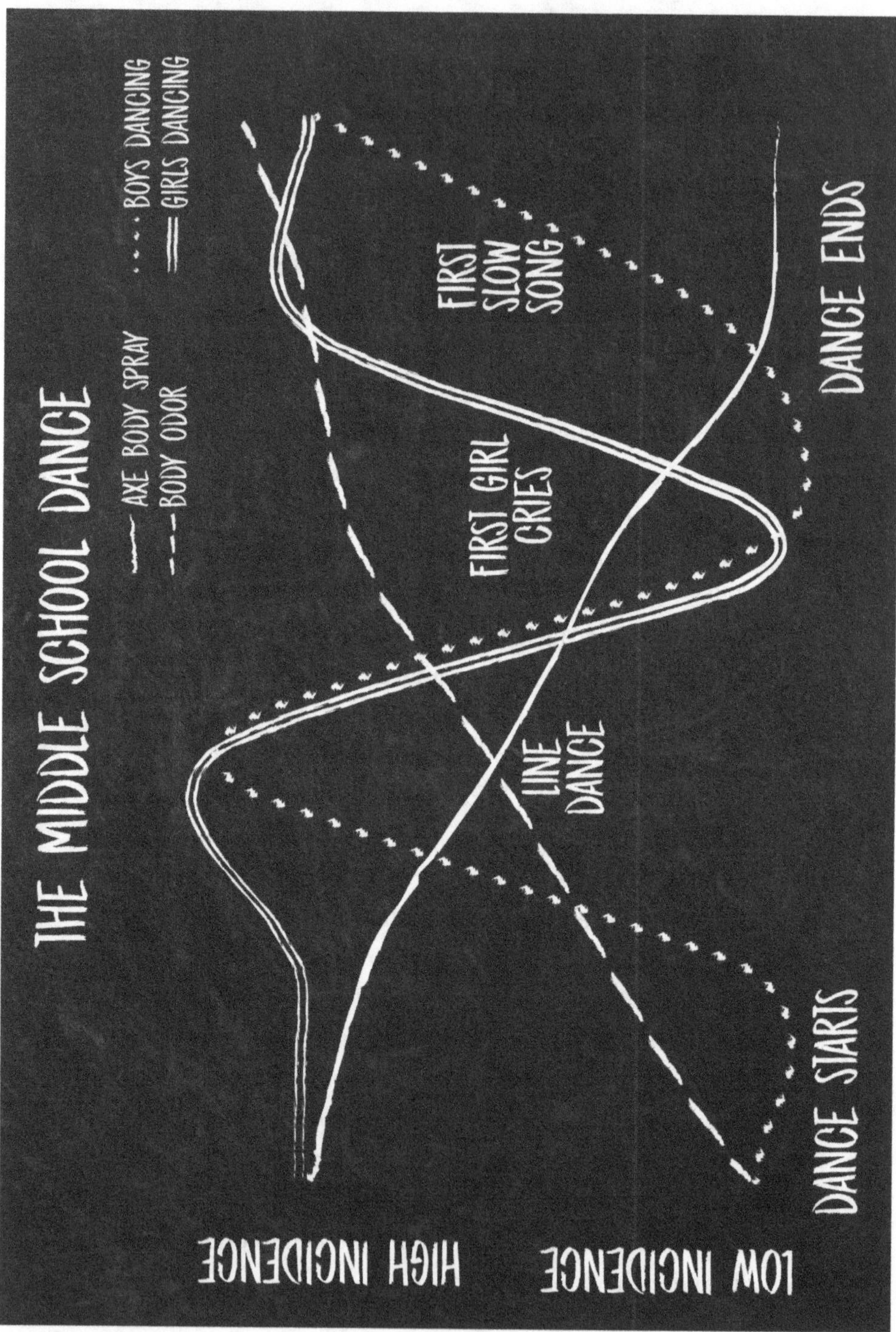
THE MIDDLE SCHOOL DANCE
AXE BODY SPRAY
BODY ODOR
BOYS DANCING
GIRLS DANCING
HIGH INCIDENCE
LOW INCIDENCE
LINE DANCE
FIRST GIRL CRIES
FIRST SLOW SONG
DANCE STARTS
DANCE ENDS

Data have flesh.

I was reminded of that one day by our middle school principal, Dave Wessel. One morning we had our regular bimonthly administrative team meeting, and the district's principals, directors, and I met for nearly four hours working on all of those things coming down the pike: Common Core State Standards, Student Growth Measures, the Ohio Teacher Evaluation System, the Ohio Principal Evaluation System, Student Learning Objectives, STAR, AIMS, and so on. Basically, they all related to three questions: What are we going to teach? How are we going to measure it? And how will we know we're doing a good job?

That afternoon I went to visit our middle school. I like to walk around seeing teachers and students in action, and I always check in at the office first. When I stopped in the office, I ran into the school principal. Mr. Wessel is a star, a true servant leader. He told me about two interactions he had had with kids that week. One was a student who was homeless and forced to live in a motel in town. The other was a student whose parent was in prison. Both students were struggling in class, which was completely understandable considering their difficult home situations. Both of these students appeared on our state report card as nothing more than a data point, a pass or a fail, a met or did-not-meet indicator. The state report card did not mention how the homeless student was doubled up in a hotel and had to share a room with five others. The state report card did not mention how the other student watched his father get arrested for domestic violence and drug trafficking.

Mr. Wessel checked in on the kids to see how they were doing, to assess how he could help, and to encourage them to keep doing their best. His concern was that all the initiatives being mandated in the name of education reform could tap our time and energy in implementing them and prevent us from "walking beside a kid and letting them know we care."

Data have flesh.

For every dot on a graph, there's a face that needs us. Sometimes kids just need an adult they can talk to. Too often they need food or clothing or shelter. For all the work that we need to do in beefing up curriculum and creating better assessments—and that is all good work—we can't forget that education happens best when a caring adult develops a trusting relationship with a kid.

Our high school's induction ceremony for the National Honor Society is always such a classy program. The choir sings, the officers give speeches, and the inductees have a candlelighting ceremony and repeat the oath. Proud parents and grandparents are in attendance. Maybe the best part is that the new inductees are allowed to invite a handful of friends to come support them as they receive their honor. Classy all around.

Now let me tell you about the worst thing I ever saw. In one place I once taught, kids who applied for induction into the National Honor Society learned if they were accepted on the same day of the induction ceremony. In fact, they learned if they had been inducted about ten minutes before the ceremony.

I'm ashamed to tell you how they found out.

All the kids who applied for the National Honor Society were told to dress in their finest for the day—shirts and ties, dresses, the whole nine yards. The kids would go to class as usual, and then minutes before the induction ceremony, current members would enter the classroom and wander around, "tapping" those who were accepted into the society.

Those tapped would immediately head to the auditorium for the ceremony.

Those untapped remained in the classroom. In their suits and ties or dresses. Humiliated.

My first experience of this was as a teacher of Honors English, where I had a class of about twenty-five students, all dressed in their Sunday best. The tappers came into my room during class, made their selections, and left with about twenty-two accepted students.

I was left in the classroom with three students, dressed in their Sunday best, fighting back tears of embarrassment and shame.

Appalled, I voiced my concern with the advisor of the club, who told me that this had always been the tradition. I was disgusted with the response, and I did not let it rest until that tradition was ended soon after. One should not perpetuate wrongdoing simply because it is the way it has always been done.

Sometimes you read in the news about college or professional athletic teams' hazing rituals, which some claim to be just a rite of passage, as if treating others inhumanely, as if embarrassing and belittling others, as if causing others humiliation or shame or physical harm is okay.

It's not okay.

It's never okay.

We must treat people in ways that maintain their dignity. Always. This is most true for those who work in professions like mine, where kids observe and absorb. A song from the musical *Into the Woods* warns about being careful about what you say and do, because children listen and see. We must hold true to our principles and be the kind of people who act as if our own mothers are always watching. Our kids deserve nothing less.

Every time I attend the National Honor Society induction ceremony in my current district, invariably my mind always returns to the prior district I worked in, where kids were humiliated so publicly. I'm proud of the district in which I currently work. One of our core values is to treat students like our own kids. That may mean tough love sometimes, but we always treat kids with dignity and respect.

PART 3

GREAT TEACHERS KNOW WHEN TO CUT THE GRASS

9

GREAT TEACHERS KNOW WHEN TO CUT THE GRASS

I was cutting my grass one August morning, grumbling to myself about how the rainy summer had pushed me to mow the lawn at least twice a week since April. And then I thought about the previous year, when the drought gave me about a six-week reprieve from mowing.

Some summers you mow a lot, and others you hardly mow at all. Isn't that exactly what good teaching is like?

In other words, good teaching is contextual. The best teachers know that no formula, no recipe, no set order of things is going to work for all kids all the time. If the grass needs cutting, you cut it. If it needs watering, you water it. If it needs aeration or grub control or any of those other tasks, that's what you do.

The best educators know that a great career will mean teaching for thirty-five years, not one year thirty-five times. No two years are the same. No two classes are the same. The best teachers understand this notion and constantly adjust strategies for instruction and motivation to get the best from each student. Those teachers who are most successful see each student as a single blade of grass and tend to each student's needs accordingly. Those who are less successful see their class as a lawn and give the same treatment to all kids, whether they need it or not.

THE BEST EDUCATORS KNOW THAT A GREAT CAREER WILL MEAN TEACHING FOR THIRTY-FIVE YEARS, NOT ONE YEAR THIRTY-FIVE TIMES.

Yes, there are some things that should never change. Great teachers have fundamental core values that are unwavering and guide them in their work. They always maintain great communication with parents. They never use sarcasm with kids. But most of all, they understand that each student is unique and should be treated as such.

This is all true for great school administrators, too. School leadership is incredibly contextual. School leadership is not as simple as enforcing a rule book. If it were, we would not need school administrators. We could hire a bunch of low-paid clerks to follow recipes instead of making complex decisions. The best school leaders know that much of what they do involves shades of gray, and their job is to take a complex situation and make the best, most reasonable decision possible for the given circumstances. And they know that a similar situation may necessitate an altogether different solution next time.

It is not easy work for either teachers or school leaders and involves a great deal of vulnerability. The best teachers and administrators have the ability to admit when they are wrong, the ability to apologize for their mistakes, and the ability to say when they don't know the answer. The worst teachers and school leaders are those who never admit a mistake, those who are going to mow the lawn whether it needs or not, all the while saying, "It's the responsibility of the grass to need cutting."

So how can we create an environment that adapts to changing times? One way is to consider what it looks like when something has run its course but also think about what it means for something to have real staying power. After all, you would not throw out the steak if a fly landed on the baked potato. Great teachers and administrators reflect often, collect data frequently, and preserve what works while making necessary changes. It is not a dichotomy of "tried and true" versus "new and exciting." There is a lot of gray, and great teachers and administrators understand what to keep and what to toss.

For example, I was driving to work one morning scanning through my SiriusXM radio when I noticed that a Madonna song was playing on '80s on 8, '90s on 9, and Pop2K at the same time. It struck me that not many artists have strung hits together for three decades in a row. Elton John. Billy Joel. U2. I'm sure there are more, but you get my point.

Now, I love one-hit wonders. Tommy Tutone's "867-5309/Jenny." Vanilla Ice's "Ice Ice Baby." The Verve's "Bittersweet Symphony." Those are all great tunes, and they take me back to a specific time and place. The artists are talented, and I enjoy their music, but eventually I get tired of hearing the same old song.

But artists like Elton John and Madonna—artists who have had hits on the charts decade after decade—have true staying power. They have been able to change with the times and always stay fresh. As a result, they have fans that span generations, and they end up on the Lake Erie shore in the Rock & Roll Hall of Fame. Great teachers are not one-hit wonders, either. To stay great, they know also that they need to constantly adapt to changing times and meet their students where their students are. So how do they do it?

Great teachers incorporate new technology into their lessons. Technology is a tool, and it will never replace great teachers. But great teachers make it a priority to learn about new technologies and how they can be used in the classroom. It would be silly for me to list technologies here because they change so rapidly. But it is safe to say that with today's students being digital natives, the classroom that I taught in twenty years ago with no computer, one overhead projector, and a blackboard would not cut it. Teachers in my district use one staff development day every year to hold their own technology miniconference. They teach their colleagues about how to incorporate new technologies in their classrooms, and the reviews are fantastic. In addition, the curriculum director, district librarian, technology director, and a few teachers collaborate to run a program called Knights of the Tech Table (Nordonia's mascot is a knight). Knights of the Tech Table sets technology challenges twice a month for every employee, including the superintendent, to work through at their own pace to earn points and prizes while learning new skills.

Great teachers constantly read and research, looking for more effective instructional methods and assessments to help their students. If you have not read an education book since college, you are committing educational malpractice. Would you go to a doctor who has not read since medical school? Of course not. Keep current with reading. While Twitter chats are great, it is irresponsible to avoid books and journals.

I recognize it is much easier to write about how to be a great teacher than it is to actually be a great teacher. Being a great teacher is the toughest job in the world. But the greatest teachers always work to stay on the charts, to not grow stale over time, and to change with the times. And the greatest teachers always know when to cut the grass and see each student as an individual blade instead of part of a lawn. Teachers owe it to themselves, they owe it to their profession, and they owe it to their kids.

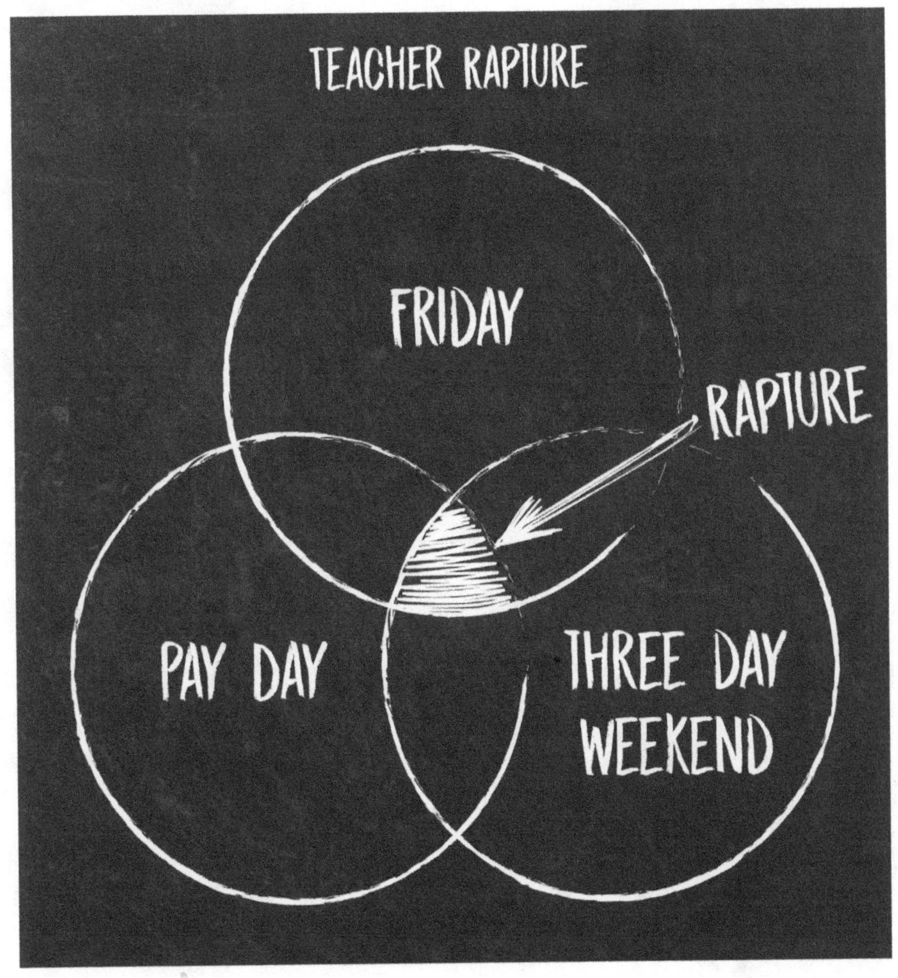

—10—

TEACHERS, LEAVE THE SARCASM IN VEGAS

After three days and nights in Las Vegas to celebrate our twentieth wedding anniversary, Amie and I arrived at the airport for an early flight home. Now, I'm not a guy who criticizes TSA agents. Their work is important, and they do a good job. But as we were going through security, we came to the end of the queue, where an agent was waiting. From here, one line separated into two, which led to the body-scan machines. We stood there, waiting to be directed to a line, when the agent said, "It's not a hard choice, guys . . . there's only two lines."

Sarcasm. *Ugh.*

We selected a line and proceeded to the scanner. Ahead of us, somebody had a bottle of water. The agent shouted to the rest of us in line: "No liquids, people. It's been banned for nine years. You think you'd know that by now."

More sarcasm. *Double ugh.*

And then somebody entered the scan machine with his belt on. The agent again shouted, "Take your belts off. I've already told you five times, but I'm sure I'll have to tell you again."

And at this point my wife begged me not to say anything to him. After all, we were tired and wanted to get home on time, and the last thing I wanted was a body cavity search. I was exhausted and broke, so admittedly I was probably easily irritated. A fabulous three-day trip with my wife had turned sour in two minutes' time.

How so? Sarcasm, hatred's ugly cousin, reared his head.

And a gentleman who could have used a pleasant tone and a smile to help weary travelers make their way through security instead decided to insult and embarrass them.

Awesome.

I was forty-three years old at the time. Educated. Successful. Confident. And the way the TSA agent was treating his customers made me furious. So imagine how students feel in a classroom when they are subject to a teacher's sarcasm.

"You forgot your pencil? What grade are you in?"

"You missed that problem on the test? I guess playing video games instead of studying wasn't a great choice."

"Jimmy. You're here today. To what do I owe this honor?"

Sarcasm isn't funny. It isn't clever. It isn't good-natured. It isn't motivational.

I know there are sarcasm proponents out there. I agree it's okay to teach sarcasm in a language arts class, and maybe even to use it when talking about my beloved Cleveland Browns when building conversational rapport with students. This very book uses a lot of sarcasm in drawing attention to some of the challenges in the world of education.

But using sarcasm as a form of motivation or discipline is never acceptable. The only thing it teaches kids is to hate school. And it not only offends and embarrasses the student who is the subject of the sarcasm but also causes those who witness it to be less likely to participate in class so they can avoid the sting as well.

Of course, there is absolutely a place for humor in the classroom. In fact, a classroom without humor is not a good place to be. A teacher using self-deprecating humor is fine. Making appropriate jokes is wonderful. A funny anecdote does wonders for building rapport. I remember Mr. Uhall, my high school chemistry teacher, telling the story about his trip to the Cincinnati Zoo, where he saw some local boys throwing "marshmellers" to the "GI-raffs." The story was legendary; I had heard it several times before from my older siblings. And that story was one of the things that made us students love Mr. Uhall.

I would like to thank the Las Vegas TSA agents for giving me that reminder that morning. (Sarcasm. *Ugh.*) I was also reminded of one other point. TSA guys work at the airport every day; they know the rules and procedures and routines. Some of us laypersons fly only once every several years, so we likely forget some of the rules and procedures and routines. Likewise, in a classroom, teachers know what's going on. It's their class. In many cases, the teachers have been there longer than the students have been alive, and they don't need to memorize six or seven different routines like the students do. So have patience with those students who incorrectly do the stuff that you think is important. Like putting their name in the wrong place. Or completing an assignment in the wrong font. Or forgetting to mark their lunch choice on the daily calendar.

Students that forget a routine should be gently and pleasantly reminded. Not reprimanded. Not disciplined. Not subjected to sarcasm. And definitely not given a reduced grade.

In other words, follow the golden rule: treat others as you'd like to be treated.

No, better yet, follow the platinum rule: treat others as *they* would like to be treated.

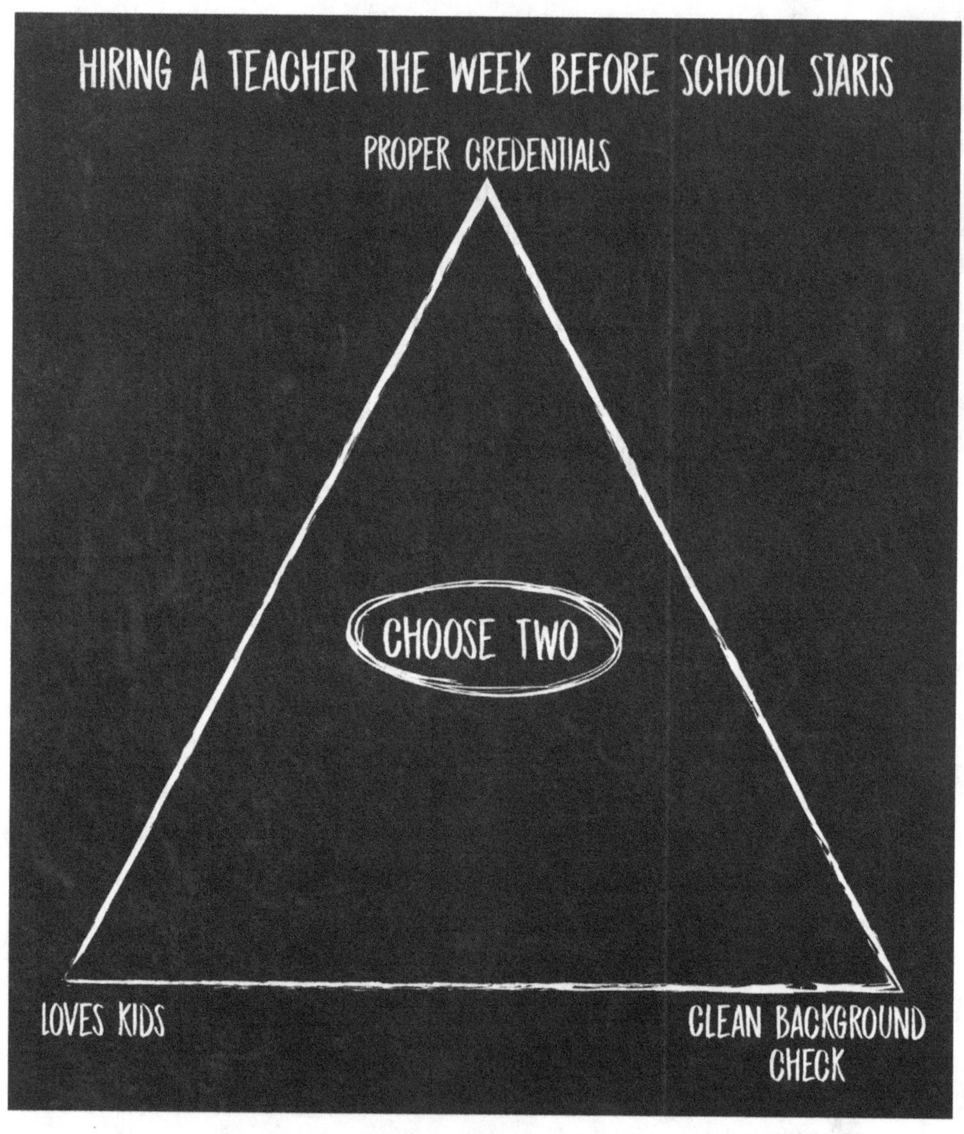
HIRING A TEACHER THE WEEK BEFORE SCHOOL STARTS
PROPER CREDENTIALS
CHOOSE TWO
LOVES KIDS
CLEAN BACKGROUND CHECK

11
A DISCOMBOBULATED THURSDAY

About halfway through my fortyish-minute drive to work, I realized I had forgotten my cell phone at home. "No sense turning around," I thought. "I'll just go one day without it."

One word: discombobulated.

I'm like many of you. I've become so accustomed to being able to check my email, tweet information, look at my calendar—even just check the time—anytime and anyplace. That day, I felt like you feel when you oversleep. Never quite right about anything. Out of place. Disconnected.

Sometimes I wonder what it was like to be a superintendent in the 1980s, before standardized tests and curriculums. Before email and voicemail. Before Twitter and Facebook. If a parent wanted to see the superintendent, they called a secretary or mailed a letter and made an appointment. Accessing school leaders—any leaders, for that matter—was so difficult, so regulated. I'm sure it was much more peaceful for those "at the top." But what did that do for the people they served?

The truth is it's so much better now. Technology has made it so that if somebody sends me an email, a tweet, or a voicemail between the hours of 6:00 a.m. and 10:00 p.m., there's about a 90 percent chance that I will see it and respond within ten minutes. Within the last year, I've called parents on Christmas Eve, Easter Sunday, and all hours of the night and day—including weekends—to respond to their questions and concerns.

It drives Amie crazy. She hates that I always have my phone on me, though I try to put it down during dinner, and I never carry it into church. But she will get used to it because she understands my philosophy that leadership is all about service. And it's impossible to serve if you can't be reached. And, frankly, for every phone call or email I respond to over the weekend, that's one less I have to worry about on Monday morning (when I'm usually grouchy about a Browns loss).

Good Luck Teaching Calendar

July

Su	Mo	Tu	We	Th	Fr	Sa
1	2	3	4	5	6	7
8	9	10	11	12	13	14
15	16	17	18	19	20	21
22	23	24	25	26	27	28
29	30	31				

August

Su	Mo	Tu	We	Th	Fr	Sa
			1	2	3	4
5	6	7	8	9	10	11
12	13	14	15	16	17	18
19	20	21	22	23	24	25
26	27	28	29	30	31	

September

Su	Mo	Tu	We	Th	Fr	Sa
						1
2	3	4	5	6	7	8
9	10	11	12	13	14	15
16	17	18	19	20	21	22
23	24	25	26	27	28	29
30						

October

Su	Mo	Tu	We	Th	Fr	Sa
	1	2	3	4	5	6
7	8	9	10	11	12	13
14	15	16	17	18	19	20
21	22	23	24	25	26	27
28	29	30	31			

November

Su	Mo	Tu	We	Th	Fr	Sa
				1	2	3
4	5	6	7	8	9	10
11	12	13	14	15	16	17
18	19	20	21	22	23	24
25	26	27	28	29	30	

December

Su	Mo	Tu	We	Th	Fr	Sa
						1
2	3	4	5	6	7	8
9	10	11	12	13	14	15
16	17	18	19	20	21	22
23	24	25	26	27	28	29
30	31					

January

Su	Mo	Tu	We	Th	Fr	Sa
		1	2	3	4	5
6	7	8	9	10	11	12
13	14	15	16	17	18	19
20	21	22	23	24	25	26
27	28	29	30	31		

February

Su	Mo	Tu	We	Th	Fr	Sa
					1	2
3	4	5	6	7	8	9
10	11	12	13	14	15	16
17	18	19	20	21	22	23
24	25	26	27	28		

March

Su	Mo	Tu	We	Th	Fr	Sa
					1	2
3	4	5	6	7	8	9
10	11	12	13	14	15	16
17	18	19	20	21	22	23
24	25	26	27	28	29	30
31						

April

Su	Mo	Tu	We	Th	Fr	Sa
	1	2	3	4	5	6
7	8	9	10	11	12	13
14	15	16	17	18	19	20
21	22	23	24	25	26	27
28	29	30				

May

Su	Mo	Tu	We	Th	Fr	Sa
			1	2	3	4
5	6	7	8	9	10	11
12	13	14	15	16	17	18
19	20	21	22	23	24	25
26	27	28	29	30	31	

June

Su	Mo	Tu	We	Th	Fr	Sa
						1
2	3	4	5	6	7	8
9	10	11	12	13	14	15
16	17	18	19	20	21	22
23	24	25	26	27	28	29
30						

○ Full moon
▲ Classroom party
⬢ First snowfall
■ Bee in classroom
▬ Testing week
□ Snow day
⬚ Day(s) before vacation
● Picture day
★ Student vomits

— 12 —

FUMBLES HAPPEN, BUT GREAT TEACHERS STICK TO THE GAME PLAN

I have almost completely kicked the habit of listening to sports talk radio. The incessant banter about steroids, Antonio Brown, the scandal of the week, and all the woeful Cleveland teams had worn on me to the point where I just could not listen anymore. Sports talk radio is a bastion of negativity, and I simply had had enough.

But I listened to some sports talk one day as I was driving home from visiting my son at school. It was a football preview show in which the hosts were discussing what each NFL team needed to do to win that day. After about fifteen minutes of listening, I came to this revelation: you could completely ignore the names of the teams they were talking about and nothing would change. The show offered cliché after cliché: The Mouthbreathers need to run the ball today. The Slobberknockers need to create turnovers. The Dinglehoppers need to protect the ball. The Knuckledraggers need to play defense.

You could say any of those things about any football team, at any level, playing anywhere in the world, and you would be right. To be a successful football team, you need to run the ball, protect the ball, play good defense, and force turnovers. They are clichés for a reason, and that reason is because they work. They are the universal game plan for winning football.

Like football, great teaching also has a universal game plan. That is, you can say certain things would be successful in any classroom in the world, at any grade level, for any ability level of student, and you would be right. To build that universal game plan, I offer these suggestions.

Build Positive Relationships with Kids

A common saying is "Kids don't care what you know until they know you care." It is imperative that you know something personal about each student, something that you can engage them in conversation about. You can tell children you care about them all you want, but displaying an understanding of their interests is much more credible. At our high school, the principals put the name of every student on the library wall. During a faculty meeting, teachers go around putting sticker dots on each student they personally know something about. When all the teachers are finished, the principals collect all the names of those students who have no dots. All these students are then assigned to an individual teacher whose responsibility it now is to make a connection with the child.

Set Expectations That Cause Students to Stretch but That Are within Their Reach

When you know your students personally, you are able to help them individualize goals that challenge them without causing frustration.

When I was sixteen, I taught myself to juggle. I did it slowly at first with only two balls. When I got better, I added a third ball. When I got better, I started going faster and throwing balls behind my back. If you had given me five balls to start, I never would have learned. Students, too, grow best when they are required to stretch but not so much that they feel hopeless.

Ensure That Students Understand the Objective of the Lesson

This is simple enough. If students do not know what they are supposed to learn, they probably will not learn it. Each lesson should begin with a discussion—not just an iteration—of the learning objectives. This includes why in addition to what. The objective should be reiterated during the lesson. You will find when students know what they are supposed to be able to do, they are more likely to accomplish it.

Assess What You Teach, Teach What You Assess

This point is all about uniformity. Have you ever taken an exam and thought to yourself, "We never covered this in class"? It was likely frustrating. Well, it is also frustrating for our students when we assess them on content that was not taught, and it is a waste of your time to teach content that will not be assessed. Of course, this teaching and assessing should be aligned to your district's adopted standards.

Use Assessments to Inform Instruction

Hopefully, you work in a district like mine that uses the Professional Learning Community (PLC) model. PLCs meet regularly to look at student assessment data and answer the single most important question: what do we do when kids don't learn? After the data are analyzed, teachers plan what they are going to do next to fill the gaps. But even if you do not work in a PLC, you should constantly be asking yourself, "What do I do next?" If you give a test that students fail, it is educational malpractice to leave those kids behind and move them on to the next unit. Teachers feel real pressure to perform and to cover too much content in too little time, but forging ahead when students don't understand is not going to make things better. Have the patience and tenacity to slow down when needed for those students who have not yet mastered the content, and be prepared to move ahead those students who have mastered it. Is that hard work? Yes, the hardest work. But each student is a blade of grass, so don't treat the class like a lawn.

Create Lessons that Engage Students

Once again, I am going to recommend Dave Burgess's *Teach Like a Pirate* for your reading pleasure. But I am also going to remind you that choice and authenticity do wonders for engagement. When kids work on real-world problems and have a choice about the types of work they are going to do, school becomes fun. Maybe not Tilt-a-Whirl-at-the-carnival fun but the kind of fun that comes from engaging in meaningful work that is going on when you look at your watch and can't believe the day is over. You do not need to reinvent the wheel to present good lessons. Project-based learning activities can be found all over the Internet; just make sure you review the activities carefully to ensure they are of quality and actually meet your standards.

Ask Great Questions

Listen to the stem in the questions you ask your students. If your questions start with "who," "where," or "when," you are probably asking questions that can easily be googled and that require low-order thinking skills. The questions you ask students, in class and on assessments, should be questions on the top end of the Bloom scale. You should be asking students to appraise, defend, evaluate, prioritize, judge, support, create, and decide. Questions with stems such as these ask students to do more than regurgitate. More challenging thinking leads to a deeper understanding of content.

Nothing in the paragraphs above is earth-shattering. We educators have been told to do each of those things a thousand times. I'm sure you can add more items to the list. If every teacher did those things in every class every day, we would be doing pretty well. But is using a universal game plan easier said than done? Absolutely. Every football team knows they have to protect the ball, but fumbles happen. Trust me; I'm a die-hard Cleveland Browns fan. I have nightmares of Earnest Byner in the 1987 AFC Championship game against Denver.

Fumbles happen.

Fumbles happen in the classroom, too. We let our sarcastic comment hurt a relationship with a student. We ask questions that too frequently are at the bottom of Bloom's taxonomy. Our students do poorly on an assessment, and we choose not to reteach to mastery. Fumbles happen.

When fumbles happen on the football field, great teams don't quit. They send out their defense and keep fighting to get the ball back. Fumbles that happen in the classroom don't stop great teachers, either. They keep following the game plan, implementing proven strategies, and reflecting on adjustments to make for tomorrow, and tomorrow, and tomorrow. Like football teams that watch postgame film, educators, too, need to reflect on our practices and never stop working to improve until every student reaches mastery.

Another way I like to think about this is by considering these questions: If students could draft their teachers like on NFL draft night, which teachers would be first-round picks? Which ones would end up as undrafted free agents? Inevitably, somebody asks if those are fair questions. After all, could we really trust students to choose their teachers? Wouldn't they choose teachers who gave easy As and no homework and simple assignments and showed movies and gave lots of free time?

Maybe some would.

But I know this. Every year, the Nordonia Schools holds its annual Superintendent's Awards, started by the brilliant Casey Wright. (You can follow Casey on Twitter at @caseygwright.) The awards go to the top graduating seniors of our high school. We enjoy dinner with their parents and honor some great kids. The coolest part of the night is when the students name and share about the school employee who made the biggest difference in their life. Often, it's a teacher. Sometimes it's a coach or aide or custodian. And when the kids speak about why they chose their most influential educator, never have I heard that they chose those educators because they were easy. Or gave little homework. Or showed movies.

Instead, the kids always talk about how their most influential educator inspired them. Challenged them to think and work harder. Encouraged them to reach for goals they never thought possible. And always, always, treated them well.

If given the choice, would some kids choose to have poor teachers? Maybe. But I trust that our kids overwhelmingly recognize the privilege of education and want to get as much out of their school years as possible.

So, teachers, there's no need to work on your forty-yard dash time. But remember that kids are counting on you to be worthy of a number-one draft pick. In football, this is typically someone who runs fast, can lift heavy weights, can throw or catch a football, and likes to physically harm other human beings. In education, the top draft picks are those who stick to the universal game plan. They treat kids well, ask great questions, align lessons and assessments, engage students, stretch students, use data to inform instruction, and ensure that students understand the lesson objectives.

So what do you think? Are you going to be drafted?

13

SOUND OF MUSIC TEACHING: A THING OF THE PAST

At one point, I had the opportunity to help our local law enforcement practice for the unthinkable, an active shooter in our schools. Officers from our local police departments (my district is made up of five distinct municipalities, so we have several sources of law enforcement) and the Metro SWAT team were on-site at our high school to practice some drills.

My role was simple. I played a staff member. My job was to go into lockdown after a PA announcement warned of an active shooter in the building. (Remember, this was a training exercise for law enforcement, not for the schools.) The officers went through several drills, stopping after each drill to debrief. It seemed to be time well spent for them. Several mentioned that they could see different ways they might improve their response, and they were anxious to go back to their departments to engage in those discussions.

The most profound comment I heard came from an officer who said, "I think we need to focus more on the goal than the procedures." In other words, the officers had a variety of protocols they were supposed to follow, but those protocols may have slowed them down from reaching the ultimate goal of securing the scene and stopping the shooter.

Those of us in the education field have seen schools transform over the years from a focus on procedures to a focus on goals. When I was a classroom teacher more than twenty years ago, we focused on content, not outcomes. My curriculum was the textbook, and my job was to get through as much of it as I could. We had no discussion about what we hoped students would accomplish by the end of the year; we just did what we could to get through the book. Proficiency testing was in its infancy, and I know that the subject matter I was teaching my ninth grade English students was different than what my colleague across the hall was teaching her ninth grade English students. We were each what I've heard someone once call "*Sound of Music* teachers." That is, we spent a lot of time teaching a few of our favorite things.

In the education field, the term we often use is *backward design*. Backward design is deciding what students are to learn before choosing the instructional methods to get there. Researchers like Jay McTighe and Grant Wiggins are experts in this philosophy and have done great work helping educators make this transition.

It only makes sense. When you are planning a trip, you know where you are going before you leave. And depending on where you are going, you might take a car or a boat or a plane or a train. You will pack differently for Florida than for Alaska, and you will pack differently for a weekend getaway than for a two-week excursion.

We need to keep in mind that before we start planning how we are going to get there, we must know exactly where it is we are going. When we know what we expect students to learn, then we can choose the proper materials and instructional strategies to help them get there. This takes a lot of work, a lot of time, and a lot of collaboration. But to me, it is so much better than where we were when I started nearly thirty years ago.

Let me share an inside glimpse into how my school district operates using PLCs. In my district, PLCs are groups of teachers of like-subjects who team up and work together to understand required content standards, coordinate the lesson plan, and create assessment analyses to measure student achievement and teacher performance.

Our teachers meet six times each year as a PLC to review the content they are teaching. These PLCs are arranged by common subject or grade areas (those who teach algebra or biology or third grade or Spanish, for example). They review their lesson plans as a group and refine testing assessments. This effort is made to evaluate if students are learning what they are expected to learn.

Most importantly, teachers are constantly asking, "What do we do when a child isn't learning?" The data gathered from the developed assessments allow teachers to reflect, revise, and reteach when necessary to help the child to improve. This effort is deliberate and totally data driven. Yes, this cycle of reflection and revision is time-consuming, but the process always gets easier, particularly through the collaborative work of PLCs. This important work is exactly what is happening in our school buildings on the six professional development days we have scheduled throughout the year when students are home from school.

Think back to when you were in high school. There were 180 days of school, and of those days, your favorite teacher probably taught 120 different lessons. If your teacher was really good, about forty of those lessons were really, really great lessons; another forty were good; and the remaining forty were probably just okay. On the days with the best lessons, your teacher left school feeling accomplished in the progress made.

There were no standardized tests, or even state content standards for that matter. If a teacher liked a particular dinosaur, they might have spent six weeks on a dinosaur unit. If a teacher liked the Civil War, they might have spent two months talking about Gettysburg. Whatever the case, back when our generation was in high school, teachers were free to teach whatever content they wanted, and they could get away with it because there were no state assessments to hold them accountable.

Then came state standards, and along with those came standardized tests. There were new expectations of what students would learn and tests to measure if they did. While the debate about standardized tests is for another book, no one can deny that one good thing to come from them is the increase in teacher collaboration, now carried out mainly within PLCs. Teachers emerged from their classrooms ready to share with, learn from, and listen to one another.

On the most basic level, PLCs provide an opportunity for teachers to take their forty really, really great lessons, combine those with another teacher's forty best lessons, and add to them yet another teacher's forty best lessons to create an entire year's worth of all-star lessons. This teamwork alone boosts student achievement.

Because we have been a PLC district for many years, our teachers are well beyond the initial phase of simply sharing lessons. On professional development days, small groups of teachers are at school in highly functional work sessions. They start by reviewing assessment data that directly correlate to state standards. They can pinpoint a specific lesson activity and determine the effectiveness in reaching its intended outcome over an entire grade level of students.

From there, they choose to reuse, revise, or recycle the activity. Data analysis of this depth can be endless, but an equally important part of a PLC day is to map the road ahead. Our PLCs plan and create lessons together, drawing on the expertise and experience of not just one teacher but three or four. They implement new research and strategies while creating in-depth, content-driven, layered lessons for our students. The teachers also ask themselves that most important question in education: "What do we do when a kid isn't learning?" From there, they create intervention strategies to promote student growth. Our teachers' plans for student achievement are targeted, intentional, and process driven.

In PLC schools like ours, teachers see progress every day, just like your favorite teacher did on a good day. The difference is, because of PLCs, our teachers know exactly when, why, and how a child's lightbulb came on. Things have come a long way since *Sound of Music* teaching. I'm glad. I'm more of a *Mary Poppins* fan anyway.

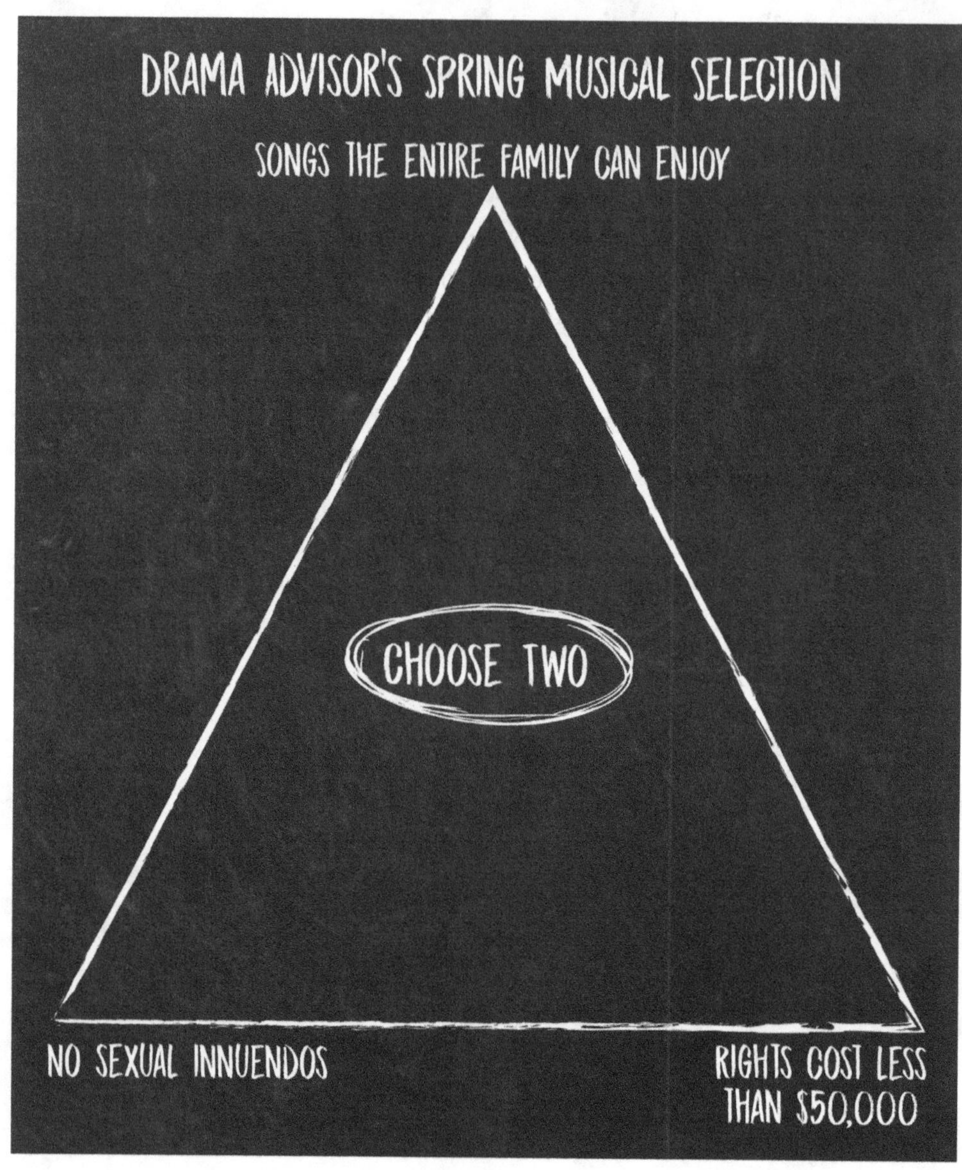
DRAMA ADVISOR'S SPRING MUSICAL SELECTION
SONGS THE ENTIRE FAMILY CAN ENJOY
CHOOSE TWO
NO SEXUAL INNUENDOS
RIGHTS COST LESS THAN $50,000

—14—

ADVICE FOR BEGINNING TEACHERS: DON'T IGNORE THE SIGNS

I was driving home from a Cleveland Indians game one night when I passed a sign on the highway stating that the left lane was closed two miles ahead. I moved to the center lane. A car pulled up beside me.

A little farther, another sign: LEFT LANE CLOSED 1 MILE AHEAD. The car was still driving next to me.

A little farther, another sign: LEFT LANE CLOSED ½ MILE AHEAD. The car was still driving next to me.

A little farther, another sign: LEFT LANE CLOSED ¼ MILE AHEAD. The car was *still* driving next to me.

You know what happened next, because it either happens to you all the time or you do it to others all the time. The left lane started coming to an end, and the car that had been driving next to me for the past two miles cut me off, sending me into a tizzy of shouting about how there had been signs warning him for TWO MILES and how could anyone be SO STUPID to IGNORE THE SIGNS and how could he HAVE A LICENSE IN THE FIRST PLACE?! It's enough to drive you crazy, isn't it? I mean, seriously, there were signs for two miles—plenty of warning—and the car still didn't do anything about it until it was too late.

We do the same things in schools sometimes, don't we? Maybe we have a student who doesn't turn in an assignment. Maybe he fails a quiz or two. Misses another assignment. Comes tardy to class. Fails a test. And before you know it, the end of the grading period is here, the student is getting a solid F, and we have not made a single effort to contact his parents to alert them that there might be a problem. Oh sure, we may have submitted grades on our web-based grading system. But is that really enough? Would we go to a doctor that made us read our own chart?

In all my years of education, I can tell you exactly how many times I've had a complaint from a parent that I communicate too much: zero. With today's technology, there is never an excuse not to have strong communication with parents through telephone, email, Twitter, web pages, and all the other ways that I don't even know about.

When we do pay attention to the signs, we quickly realize that there's something unique about every student. Our focus needs to be on trying to find that unique quality and helping them to bring it out. We must give each student the individual attention needed to identify and cultivate his or her gifts. That task is not always easy, as all of us have gifts that run the spectrum.

Take me, for example. Everybody loves to know a guy with a Santa suit. How do I know? I know because *I* have a Santa suit. I bought it several years ago when I was involved in community theater, and people who know I have the suit frequently either ask me if they can borrow the suit or if I can play Santa for them at a party or family event.

Everybody also loves to know a deejay. This I know from experience as well. Having deejayed for many, many years, I get repeated requests from friends or acquaintances to play at parties they are throwing or to put playlists together for them. I haven't deejayed regularly for many years, yet throughout any given year I get at least half a dozen requests to help somebody out.

Everybody loves to know someone with a truck. This I do *not* know from experience. I know it because *I* love knowing people with trucks. I don't want to own a truck, but I am not afraid to ask a friend to borrow a truck if I have firewood to haul or furniture to move, which seems to be at least a few times a year.

While we might grumble a little bit about people looking to get something from us, the truth is we like it. It feels good to be needed, to have a gift that allows us to make others' lives better.

As educators, our job is to help our students find *their* Santa suit.

Each of our students comes to us with a gift, a talent, a skill that is often yet unknown to them. Helping them find the gift—helping them find a passion for doing something they are good at—is, to me, what education is all about. When kids find that something, they are set on a path that practically guarantees success.

Earlier I wrote of some tangible ideas to help students find their solo. That same advice holds true here. We need to offer students a variety of course options, clubs, field trips, and other experiences. But also, we need to constantly support and encourage our students, to let them know they are capable of more than they believe, to tell them that somewhere within them is something special, something they will be happy doing and others will be happy that they do.

Michelangelo said, "Every block of stone has a statue inside it and it is the task of the sculptor to discover it." Educators are sculptors, too. Every day we have the opportunity to see the signs that are right in front of us and to help kids uncover the beautiful statue inside themselves. Our students have gifts that will change the world. Let us do everything we can to help our students discover their talents—talents far more valuable than a Santa suit.

15

WANTED: GREAT TEACHERS AND GREAT EMPLOYEES

Every year, in the midst of hiring season, I interview many candidates hoping to land a teaching job with us. The ideal candidate—in addition to having the ability to walk on water—teaches dynamic lessons, differentiates instruction, communicates with students' families, uses formative assessment to guide instruction, develops great relationships with students, knows how to integrate technology into the classroom, and exhibits extensive professional commitment.

Most teaching candidates know about this laundry list, of course, and they come to interviews prepared to answer questions related to these topics. Some candidates seem more sincere than others, some more nervous, some have had unique experiences, and some seem to have a deeper understanding of these ideas than others. But overall, it is rare to find a candidate who doesn't understand what it takes to be a good teacher. (Now, putting it into practice is another matter entirely.)

But being a good teacher doesn't necessarily mean a person is going to have a successful thirty-five-year career. Consider this: assuming a teacher works for thirty-five years, and factoring in salary and benefits, each new hire is potentially a $3 to 4 million investment for a school board. Realizing this, districts look to hire folks that are going to be not only dynamic in the classroom but also good colleagues. In other words, it is not enough to be a great teacher; one must also be a good employee.

What does that mean? It means that teachers who interview need to realize that hiring decisions are often made based on much more than what is said in the interview. Other types of valuable information also help to inform a hiring decision:

- How well did the candidate treat the secretary who scheduled the interview? If the candidate was rude or arrogant on the phone, it is a red flag that he or she will be rude and arrogant to colleagues as well. They say people who are not nice to waiters are not nice people. I agree. Similarly, people who treat secretaries as if they are not as important as certified staff are pompous and not welcome on my team.
- How responsive was the candidate to returning phone calls or emails to schedule the interview? It is important to provide great instruction, but teachers also have many deadlines they need to meet for the district to run smoothly. This requirement is even more true for teachers of students with disabilities. Those teachers have federal mandates for record keeping. If it takes the candidate multiple days or attempts to get scheduled for the interview, it is a red flag for meeting deadlines when on staff, which would be annoying at best and possibly cause due-process complaints at worst.
- How well did the candidate treat the receptionist who welcomed him to the interview? Just like the secretary who scheduled the interview, the receptionist who welcomes the candidate should be treated well. The candidate should

smile and be pleasant, ask about the receptionist's day, and try to make small talk. If a candidate is rude, I will learn of it and cross him or her off my list.

- How prompt was the candidate to the interview? Absent a legitimate excuse (e.g., a flat tire), the candidate needs to arrive at the interview early. Teachers do not have the luxury that other professionals might have to be a few minutes late to work. If a teacher is late, a classroom of kids goes unsupervised, and that can't happen.
- How professional did the candidate appear? Times have changed with regards to tattoos and jewelry and hairstyles. What has not changed is the candidate needs to be clean and well-groomed and dressed in professional clothing a step above what they would wear to work. Sometimes I see new college graduates wearing what I am sure is their only suit, and it may not fit right. I never hold that against them. I would rather see a candidate in a suit too small or too large than one in khakis and a golf shirt.
- How much did the candidate research about the place he may be working for the next thirty-five years? I always ask the candidates what they found in their research about us that makes them think they would want to work here. They need an answer with details that proves they at least took the time to try to learn something. I am not looking for accuracy of answers; I am looking to see that they spent the time to do a little extra work.
- How likely does it appear that the candidate will be able to work well with others, to be part of a team, and to be a positive ambassador for the district to others in the community? Candidates need to have a good sense of self. That means they need to know when they are talking too much or coming off as arrogant. In my district, we work in teams, and nobody wants to work on a team on which somebody hogs

the time or appears condescending. In my district, lack of interpersonal skills is one of the reasons why most otherwise-qualified candidates do not get hired.

As I've said elsewhere, great teachers know they should teach thirty-five different years, not one year thirty-five times. And after that career, each teacher will have a retirement party. At that retirement party, all the guests will be happy. If you have been a good employee, the guests will be happy *for* you retiring. If you haven't been a good employee, they will be happy *because* you are retiring.

When hiring teachers, I always look for those that have the skills to be great performers in the classroom. But to get a job with us, candidates need to show that they will be not only a great teacher but also a great employee. They need to show up on time, look professional, be friendly to everyone, and have a good sense of how to interact in a conversation. If a person has strong teaching skills but lacks the other qualities, it is likely he or she will not get a job in my district. When I decide to make a potential multimillion-dollar investment in a new hire, that candidate has to check all the boxes.

PART 4

DON'T WRITE THE REVIEW UNTIL YOU WATCH THE MOVIE

On Kindness, Community, and Diversity

—16—

CHOOSE KINDNESS: MY MESSAGE FOR NEW TEACHERS

Each year we hold a new-teacher orientation for our most recently hired staff members. It is always a privilege to be with this group of excited professionals looking to build a fabulous career. Much of the orientation is basic information: when you get paid, how you call out sick, what you should do if your ceiling springs a leak. All the central office administrators talk to the group about their responsibilities and the circumstances that might call for the new teachers to contact the central office staff.

I always speak last. I have met all the new hires during the interview process, but this is my one time to address them as a group, the one chance I have to tell them what it really means to work in our district. I remind them why they were selected to work with us, and I tell them my expectations for all the things not directly related to curriculum and instruction. In other words, I spend most of my time telling them how I expect them to treat our kids.

Why Are You Here?

First, I ask, "Why are you here?" Someone always answers, "To teach." And then I repeat my question: "No. I mean, why are *you* here?"

I tell the new teachers that we had thousands of applications and conducted hundreds of interviews for the positions those folks were hired to fill. We are a destination district: we hire a lot of teachers from other school districts, and when they join us, they rarely leave. So what is it that we saw in them that made us want to make them part of the team?

I inform them that I didn't hire them because I thought they fit the Nordonia Way. In fact, I say, the Nordonia Way is only about getting better. So they were not hired because they fit our mold; instead, we hired them because we saw something in them that we wanted to become more like. They are talented and professional, and we hope to learn from them and benefit from their talents. But more than that, their interviews showed us that they have the abilities and dispositions to treat kids well, to persevere, to work on a team, to continue to grow professionally. In short, they exhibit what we call *extensive professional commitment*, a term coined in the book *Supportive Supervision*.

The Greatest Miracle in the World

Next, I tell the new teachers about a book I read in ninth grade, a book by a man named Og Mandino called *The Greatest Miracle in the World*. Mandino wrote, "The surest way to doom yourself to mediocrity is perform only the work for which you are paid." That quote is one I have remembered every day of my life since. I have it hanging up in my office, and I give every new teacher the quote printed on a piece of card stock for their own classrooms.

I ask how many of them are hoping to have a long, average career. No hands go up. I ask how many of them want to have a long, awesome career. And all the hands are in the air. I repeat the Mandino quote and remind them that the only way their career will be better than mediocre is to give more than is expected. That sometimes means missing a lunch to tutor. It means attending their students' games and concerts. It means joining committees. It means developing a unique communication system for parents or inviting them into the classroom to participate in activities. It means everything other than showing up when the first bell rings and heading out when the last bell rings.

Easiest Job in the World

At new-teacher orientation, I tell our new staff that being a mediocre teacher can be the easiest job in the world. By being nice to kids and not making waves, the mediocre teacher can coast through a long career, even with awful instruction. Principals are far too busy to be able to deal effectively with mediocre teachers. Horrible teachers (those who are mean to kids, who have attendance problems, who can't get along with colleagues, who act inappropriately) are likely to be addressed by administration, but it is almost unheard of for a teacher to lose a job only because of poor instruction. Principals may pressure mediocre teachers come evaluation time, but a tenured mediocre teacher can have a long, riskless career.

On the other hand, being a great teacher is the hardest job in the world. Great teachers differentiate instruction, put in long hours, worry about their students, facilitate awesome learning activities, give meaningful assessments, let the results of the assessments drive their instruction, and so much more. You can have a long career of mediocrity and never be noticed. But the great ones take risks, make mistakes, and keep trying. Great teachers stay current with research and constantly modify lesson plans to meet students' needs. Mediocre teachers keep the same lesson plans year after year without changing a thing, despite the fact that students have different needs.

When I attended the open house for my oldest son when he was in high school (I live in a district different from the one I work in), his math teacher gave us parents a calendar that showed every homework assignment for the year. While she may think that making that calendar made her great and proactive, that to me was the epitome of mediocre. How could a teacher possibly know what the students would need to be doing in three days, let alone six months? It was lazy and irresponsible, but she was at the end of a long career. Mediocre is easy and brings little stress.

Every year I remind my new teachers that they did not get into this profession to doom themselves to mediocrity. They want to be great, so they need to put forth the effort.

The Second Fisherman

At their orientation I give all the new employees a copy of the poem "The Second Fisherman." I found the poem on a little card in 1988 and kept it in my wallet until my oldest son went off to college, when I passed it on to him. You can see the card's wrinkles from spending twenty-five years in my pocket.

I read the poem to the new staff and remind them that teaching is a mission. School is literally a life-or-death proposition for some students. Some may have a great chance of success because of their family circumstances, but others' only chance literally rests on the quality of their education.

I grew up poor. I was the youngest of eleven, and my mom stayed home for most of my childhood. We lived in a modest house. I shared a bedroom with three brothers; two of us slept on the top

THE SECOND FISHERMAN:

A PARABLE

a fisherman on a river bank
at the bottom of a hill
saw a drowning child

he jumped in to save him

soon there was another
and another and
he was quickly overwhelmed

a second fisherman
seeing this
climbed to the top of the hill
so that he could stop them

from falling in

Compliments of
Rubber City Printery, Inc.

bunk, and two on the bottom bunk. We were on the free-lunch program and received government cheese.

My dad was a hard worker, running presses at a small rubber company in Akron, working double shifts. Dad would go to work, come home for dinner, then go back to work. Eventually, he made his way into management. In 1977, my dad (and his twin brother) was laid off from his job. (In the photo, which appeared in the local paper, my dad is on the right, my Uncle Don on the left.) I can't imagine the fear he must have faced, an unemployed father of eleven. For most of my older siblings, education was the only way they were going to be able to better themselves. There was no safety net for them. If they did not do well in school, they would be forced to find manufacturing jobs, which were disappearing in our part of the country in the 1970s.

But by the time I was in high school, my dad had found a new job at a different rubber company and ended up buying the business. He eventually added a few more small businesses and was doing quite well. Unlike my older siblings, I always had the luxury of knowing that if I failed out of college, I could always find a good job working for my dad.

Many, many students, though, do not grow up with the privilege I had. For many, literally the only opportunity they will ever have to find a job with health care and a pension comes from the quality of education they receive. We can't give up on any student, ever. When I read the poem, I see the first fisherman as all those social service organizations that do noble work helping those in need. But teachers need to be the second fisherman. We have to stop the kids from falling into the abyss in the first place.

Riding the Train

During new-teacher orientation, I also tell the new staff about one of the scariest things that ever happened to me.

When our kids were young, Amie and I took our boys to Washington, DC, for our family vacation. Everyone should get to DC. It's such a great city, and the sense of history and patriotism you feel there is indescribable. Our hotel was outside the city, and we rode the Metro into town each day for our activities. That summer was one of the hottest on record—near or over one hundred degrees every day we were there.

We spent one particular day walking all over the city seeing all sorts of sights. By late afternoon we were hot, tired, hungry, and ready to ride the Metro back to the hotel for a dip in the pool and some dinner. We walked into the Metro station and bought our fare cards, then had to ride an escalator down to the loading platform.

Our youngest, Matthew, was first on the escalator. I was directly behind. Amie and Isaac pulled up the rear.

As we got about halfway down the escalator, I could see our train arrive. The doors opened as people piled off the train. At this point we were near the bottom of the escalator, and when we reached the bottom, I hurried Matthew onto the train. I turned around to see Amie and Isaac still coming down the escalator, and then turned back to the train to see Matthew on board.

Then I saw the doors start to close.

Instinct took over and I jumped between the closing train doors. They sort of smashed me in my ample belly, but I was able to squeeze through to get aboard. I looked out the window to see Amie and Isaac still standing on the platform as our train pulled away.

A few text messages later, Amie and I figured out that Matthew and I would get off at the next stop and wait for the others to catch up with us. The rest of the ride was silent. I'm not sure what was going through everyone else's minds, but what was going through mine was the terror of almost having been separated. But more than that, I was thinking about how terrified Matthew would have been had he been alone on that train.

We have kids alone on the train every day in American schools. These are kids who come from backgrounds of poverty, or abuse, or neglect, or any other varied traumas, and often a combination of traumas. These are kids who have lost parents, who haven't eaten, who have spent the previous night taking care of their little brothers and sisters because there was no adult at home.

Imagine the fear these kids have, these kids who are alone on the train. They do not have the support system so many of us take for granted. They are alone on the train, and they so desperately need us to ride with them. We must hop on board with them. That may mean connecting families with area social resources to make sure a student has a coat for the winter or food on the weekend. It may mean lending an ear when a student had a domestic issue the night before or finding counseling services for the student and parents. It may mean not reprimanding a student who falls asleep in class because of being up all night. Most educators have studied American psychologist Abraham Maslow's work and understand his belief that we must attend to students' primary needs before we can ever hope to educate them.

Let me tell you about one of our teachers who rode the train. A few years ago, we were honoring our retirees at the end-of-the-year convocation day. At the ceremony, colleagues traditionally get on stage and speak about the retirees, telling stories from their career. When a teacher got up to speak about one of our retirees, what she said put me in tears. As the story went, this retiring kindergarten teacher had, for most of her career, tape recorded herself reading children's stories. Then, when she knew she had a student whose parents were not reading to their child at home, the teacher would buy the student a small cassette player and send home some of the tapes she had recorded. The teacher wanted to make sure none of her students went to sleep without a good-night story.

Kids Won't Follow Rules in May

. . . because you told them the classroom rules in August. I spend time at new-teacher orientation every year advising the new staff about how they should spend their first few days of school. Too often, teachers are concerned with spending the first days going over the rules and procedures, thinking that setting a good tone early will help maintain a disciplined classroom all year. Wrong. Again, kids will not follow the rules in May because you told them the rules in August. They will follow the rules in May if you spent time in August building relationships and trust.

Yes, it is fine to teach some of the procedures kids need to follow, such as where to put their coats and where their seats will be. But the first several days of school are better spent interacting with students and learning their interests. One absolute is getting to know the students' names on the first day, which will necessitate playing some name games. Take time to ask questions of the students: what they like to do outside of school, what their favorite subject in school is, what type of work they prefer doing, what type of work has caused them struggles in the past. Learn as much as you can about your students, and also let them learn about you. Giving students a glimpse into your personal life helps break down barriers and allows them to see you as a real person.

In the first few days it is also important to get busy teaching, and make sure you give an early assignment that allows all kids to be successful. Kids are going to be nervous; they are in a new grade with a new teacher, maybe even in a new school. They are worried that things will be tougher than last year, and they wonder if this is the year that the bottom falls out and they aren't able to keep up. Of course, those fears are unfounded, so give kids a chance to be successful right away so their worries can be put to rest.

For most kids in grades five and up, their biggest worries are what the best restroom is to use, how their lock works, and who they will sit with at lunch. Work with your colleagues to develop programs to address these items right away. Maybe that means running a ten-minute practice lunch first thing in the day and helping kids practice opening their locks. Whatever you can do to minimize stress will build trust with your students and allow for a more successful year.

Hero or Villain?

I was once invited to speak to the CYO Camp Christopher Day Camp staff to prepare them for their upcoming season. I spent ten summers at Camp Christopher as a counselor, bus driver, and camp director, and I was honored to be invited back.

I am a huge supporter of summer camps. Every kid should spend time in the wilderness making friends and getting muddy. Summer camp teaches life lessons in teamwork, leadership, spirituality, environmentalism, fitness, and so much more. I loved swimming, canoeing, horseback riding, hiking, crafts, games, singing songs . . . the list is endless.

One of the best parts of Camp Christopher for me was the storytelling. Every camp has its own stories and legends, and Camp Christopher was no different. "Old Man's Cabin," "Mummy's Cave," "Frankenstein's Chair," and "The Man Walking Backwards"—these were all stories that we loved to tell campers, and it was fun to see over the years how the stories changed, much like the oral tradition of centuries ago. The stories we told all featured interesting characters—some heroes, some villains—who came to life for our campers as they had for campers from previous generations.

In that speech, I reminded the day camp staff of something I like to remind our teachers of at new-teacher orientation. That is, you will be a character in the life story of each child with whom you interact. Whether you are a hero or a villain or even a nondescript extra is entirely up to you. When you work with kids, every day you make a difference in their lives. You can encourage them to reach for their dreams or dissuade them from taking risks. You can treat them with warmth and compassion or coldness and animosity. When they make mistakes, you can show them mercy or vindictiveness. You can speak to them with kindness and politeness or sarcasm and harshness. You can challenge them to reach heights they never knew possible or undermine them with low expectations.

One thing is certain when you work with kids. Twenty years from now, they will tell stories about the time they spent with you. In their stories, will you be a hero or a villain? It really is up to you.

Don't Write the Review until You Watch the Movie

By sharing this story at orientation, I inform our new teachers about reserving judgment. One Saturday night, Amie, our son, and I went to see the movie *The Monuments Men*. It was a decent movie but not nearly as memorable as what happened to us during the film.

As soon as the movie started, my wife pointed out a young man seated one row in front and about ten seats to the left of us using his iPhone to record the movie. Despite having his face almost pressed against his phone, clearly his camera was on and the movie was on his screen.

I was furious.

First, the light from the camera was distracting. Second, I've heard about these guys—these pirates—who film movies on the opening weekend and sell them on the Internet. I remember Kramer and Jerry doing such a thing on an episode of *Seinfeld* many years back.

I was so angry, both at the distracting light from the young man's phone and his audacity to commit a crime in such a conspicuous way, that I went to the lobby to report him to the manager. Of course, when I came back to the auditorium, the young man had put his phone away.

I knew his temptation would get the best of him, so I sat waiting. And waiting. And waiting.

And about ten minutes later, when the movie was using subtitles for the second time, the young man turned his camera on again and nearly pressed his face against the screen. I couldn't believe it and actually considered throwing a Junior Mint at him.

And then Amie whispered, "I think he has a vision problem. I don't think he can see the subtitles."

Ugh.

It suddenly became clear to me that was exactly what he was doing. He was trying not to distract the rest of us in the auditorium, and he was staring at the image on his phone so he could read the subtitles and just enjoy the film.

Suddenly, the light coming from his phone didn't seem as distracting to me.

And just as suddenly, I felt like an idiot.

And about ten minutes later, when a police officer came into the auditorium to ask him to turn off his phone, I felt even more like an idiot.

The young man's father told the police officer what was happening. The police officer apparently then told the manager, who returned a few minutes later with some sort of magnifying glasses for the young man to wear for the rest of the show.

And for the rest of the show, I sat thinking about how they should really have some way for people with disabilities to have a pleasurable viewing experience and make accommodations for them and so on and so forth. But really, I sat thinking about how ashamed I was to rush to judgment on this young man, to condemn him in my mind before I really had any idea what was going on.

And then I thought about how that happens in classrooms sometimes. A student is rude. Or disruptive. Or doesn't do his work. Or smarts off. Or falls asleep. Or is distracted. And so often our initial reaction is disgust or frustration or anger. We want to shake these students until they sit up straight and shut their mouths and do their work. But often the students who cause the most anxiety are actually the ones who need our love the most. Maybe their parents are going through a divorce. Maybe they are hungry. Maybe they are caring for siblings while their parents are working. Maybe there are drugs or neglect or abuse or any other number of dysfunctional situations in the home.

You have heard it said that we must always be kind because everyone is fighting a battle you know nothing about. Not just your family or friends or strangers in movie theaters. But kids.

In your classroom. Every day.

How many times do we make judgments about people without having all the information? We might criticize their ability, their integrity, their honesty, their intentions, and so often we are way off base in our perceptions. Too often our first instinct is to look for what somebody did wrong, when we should reflect on the words of Stephen Covey ("Seek first to understand, then to be understood"). Or St. Francis of Assisi ("O master grant that I may not so much seek . . . to be understood as to understand"). Or consider Atticus Finch, who said, "You never really understand a person until you consider things from his point of view . . . until you climb into his skin and walk around in it."

That Saturday reminded me that it is easy to come to judgment—that it is easy to decide that some people are bad or worthless or lazy—without ever really knowing their story. In other words, don't write the review before you watch the entire movie.

As professional educators, let's do everything in our power to avoid falling into that trap. Talk to kids. Get to know them. Try to understand what battles they are fighting. To put it another way, ruminate on another Covey quote: "We judge ourselves by our intentions and others by their behavior." We should all work harder to look at intentions and seek first to understand. And then, when you do understand, follow Maya Angelou's advice and be the rainbow in their cloud.

Harley or Scooter, Same Destination

One final message for our new teachers is this: in case there was any doubt, I am officially uncool. I bought a scooter. It's a tiny little 50cc

Honda Metropolitan. If you're like me, you have no idea what *50cc* means. What it translates to in real life is this: If the wind is at my back and I'm going downhill, I can go forty miles per hour. If I'm going uphill and you're behind me, just hope you're not in a hurry.

I'm not Motorcycle Guy. Motorcycles scare me to death. I will never own a motorcycle. But I love my scooter. I ride it to the park, where I like to take hikes. And I ride it to the grocery store as long as I am only buying something smaller than a watermelon, which is about all the "trunk" under the seat can hold. My scooter is fun. And it gets 110 miles per gallon. And did I say I love it?

One day I was at the gas station—where I filled the tank for $3.25—when a guy on a Harley pulled up. His bike was big. And loud. And powerful. And he gave me a look that told me he knew his bike was big and loud and powerful, and my scooter was small and weak. He didn't need to give me that look; I know my scooter is small and weak. But here's the thing: he drove his big, loud, powerful Harley to the gas station, and I drove my small, weak scooter to the gas station. And there we were, both at the exact same place at the exact same time.

That is school, my friends. Some kids ride to school on a Harley. Their "Harley" is a library of books at home, food on the table, a stable family situation, experiences at museums and concerts, and a myriad of other advantages we pray all kids could have.

Other kids ride to school on a scooter. And still other kids walk to school barefoot.

Our job is to get all the kids to the gas station, no matter what kind of bike they are riding or not riding. The "gas station" is college and career readiness.

No doubt, it is hard work. But we can't give up on any kids. We need to do whatever we can to get them there. For some kids, the trip will take more time. Some kids will need more road signs than others. Some kids we may have to push or tow. And some will use their

Harley to go much farther than the gas station. But until we get every student ready to go to college or start a career, we must not rest.

IF YOU ARE EVER WONDERING WHAT THE RIGHT THING TO DO IS, CHOOSE KINDNESS.

As I finish my storytelling at new-teacher orientation each year, I take some time to pull it all together. I tell a lot of stories with a lot of different messages, but the one common theme is this: be kind. If you are ever wondering what the right thing to do is, choose kindness. Life is hard enough as it is. Sometimes adults forget how hard it was to be a kid. We romanticize about cartoons and summer breaks and no bills to pay, conveniently forgetting the real struggle of making friends, of family challenges, and of problems we cannot control. You have heard it said that everyone you know is fighting a battle you know nothing about. Well, that includes kids. So when you are responsible for a classroom of thirty boys and girls, your first priority must always be to be kind.

17

EVERY DAY WE TEACH THEM WELL: THE IMPORTANCE OF COMMUNITY

We cannot go a day without hearing of an awful tragedy in some part of the world, sometimes in our own state or community. But I'm not swayed by the headlines. I still believe the world is a good place filled with good people. I still believe the world has more generosity than greed. More mercy than vindictiveness. More acceptance than rejection. More upstanders than bullies. More givers than takers. More people who know what is right, and who fight for what is right, and who spend every minute of every day doing what is right.

But for those times when it seems like maybe evil is winning, that is when I am so proud to be part of my school district. I am proud to work with a staff who cares about kids—a staff who doesn't just provide a great education but who also provides food and clothing and guidance and support to any child in need. I'm proud to work in a community where parents and community members are proud of our schools and who give of their own time and resources to help our staff help our kids. And I'm proud of our kids. They're kids, and they can make some mistakes sometimes. Good grief, don't we all? But when the rubber meets the road, our kids care for each other, and they care for their education, and they genuinely want to grow up into responsible, caring adults.

I will never forget Monday, January 11, 2016. I had just gotten home from a long day at work, sometime after nine. because we had a board meeting that night. I got a call from one of our elementary school principals who told me the home of one of our students had exploded a little while ago. It turned out to be worse than that.

The father, Jeffrey Mather, had poured gasoline throughout the home before setting it on fire, causing an explosion. He was found dead next to a charred gas can.

His wife, Cynthia Mather, was also found dead in the home. The medical examiner noted that her cause of death was an overdose of Prozac, but it was unclear whether it was murder or suicide. They knew she was dead before the fire, though, because there was no indication of smoke inhalation.

The two children found died of suffocation, though the Summit County medical examiner was unable to tell how they suffocated. Alyson Mather, 12, and Ruthie Mather, 9, were dead before the smoke from the fire would have filled their lungs. Ruthie was one of our students; Alyson had also been with us but was currently being homeschooled.

Medical examiner records said their task of finding out how the family died was complicated by how burned their bodies were. However, it was determined the father set the fire on the first floor of the home. The other three were on the second floor of the home when the fire started. They fell through the second floor when it collapsed.

The medical examiner could not determine which parent was responsible for the death of the children, though the father had previously attempted suicide in December after his role changed at his job. He told authorities then that he had been depressed for a few months.

News that the fire was not accidental shocked the community, and we in the schools were devastated by the death of Ruthie Mather, a second grader in our system. Ruthie was smart, sweet, kind, and a wonderful artist. She was adored by teachers and classmates, and she loved coming to school. We still miss her terribly.

In times of tragedy, though, heroes emerge. The safety forces in our community do incredible work under horrible conditions, and they should be praised for their professionalism and calmness in the face of chaos. The entire elementary school staff did incredible work helping their students and each other through the initial stages of the grieving process. Many staff members from other buildings offered amazing support as well.

Losing a student is a school leader's worst nightmare. The kids we work with every day are like our own. We are their surrogate mothers and fathers, and we are in a profession that has unbelievable highs and heartbreaking lows. The community should know how truly dedicated and caring the Nordonia Schools staff is. They are generous and empathetic and caring.

We also saw an outpouring of compassion and generosity from our community. A sampling of unsolicited emails I received in the hours following the tragedy show the mercy of this community.

From a health-care worker: "Absolutely devastating. As you know, I work for Hospice of the Western Reserve and we have a school crisis team—we absolutely can send someone out ASAP if you need additional resources. Please let me know as this is the least I can do until you let us parents know what else is needed."

From a local minister: "Hi, Dr. Clark. I am the lead pastor at Western Reserve Grace Church here in Macedonia, writing to offer our help to come alongside you and your staff during this time of loss for students and families in light of the tragedy in Northfield. I have a family ministries staff that covers the ages of birth through high school. Myself and my team offer to be at your disposal. I have no agenda other than authentically seeking to offer our encouragement and help. Please feel free to call me personally if we can help in any way. Praying for you, Dr. Clark. Leading through times like this is tough . . . I get it."

From the senior pastor at United Methodist Church: "I am grateful for your concern, Joe; of course, you can call on me if necessary for any help. Situations like this make me thankful for many things, one of which is knowing the staff and faculty in our schools are caring, involved, compassionate, and helpful. You all go far beyond academics. Lynn and I thank God for you regularly."

From the manager of Chick-fil-A: "Hi, Joe. I heard about the tragedy in Northfield this morning—I want to help, please let me know what we can do. I know this is a hectic time, but when you have the opportunity, please call me at the restaurant or on my cell phone. In the meantime, my leadership and I will be praying." Chick-fil-A then provided lunch for the school's staff members for two days.

Each of us goes through life with critics. Some of our critics are more vocal or visible than others, but as they say, there is always a guy in the crowd making fun of the hero's shirt. While critics might need to look for the right time to throw stones, there is never a wrong time to be kind. And the truth is our community is full of kind, caring, compassionate people, people who go out of their way to help others in need.

Some people see the donut, and some people see the hole. I see the donut. When I retire a long time from now, I'm going to remember all the wonderful people I worked with and the community I served. Our community is a fabulous place. We should be proud of our community and proud of our schools. But after this tragedy, I decided that it shouldn't take tragedy to keep that in mind. After the news came out, colleagues across the state sent me emails and texts offering their sympathy. I was grateful for their support, but my response is always the same: every day 3,600 kids come to our schools, and every day we teach them well and treat them well, and every day I feel blessed to be a part of their lives.

And when you hang out with these kids, you realize pretty quickly that the future of the world is bright. Notwithstanding media accounts, kids today are more compassionate and accepting than at any other time in history.

In the case of another tragedy close to our community, a neighboring school district had two student suicides recently. In response, a group of our own fifth grade students thought it would be a good idea to show unity in the wake of recent events in the nearby community by telling our neighbors how much they matter. When their students entered the school one morning, they were greeted with a personal message, written on a sticky note and stuck on their lockers, the messages showing the grieving students how important each is to all of us.

The principal of that school wrote to me to say, "I cannot begin to tell you how much this effort warms my heart. Our kids are compassionate and strong and remind me constantly how blessed we are to have them in our lives. Let's celebrate how much our kids mean to us through the work of a small group of fifth grade students and their caring for our school and community."

As school leaders, it is good to know that a community will have your back in times of tragedy. But we should never forget the importance of the community to our schools in all times. Sometimes I hear arrogant school leaders dismiss community members as not deserving to be a part of the school's operations. The thinking goes, "I am the educated expert, so why should I listen to those who are not as qualified as me?" That's a fool's belief.

For school leaders who want to build relationships with the community, it is imperative to remember who owns the schools. While my position as superintendent grants me much statutory and positional power, the way I view my position is as just another member of a larger team. The community owns the schools. My job as superintendent is to serve the community's wants and needs, not my own.

As a professional educator, I naturally have a depth of knowledge and experience that many community members do not have. I have a responsibility to give professional advice and opinions on what best practices may be in any given situation. But when it comes down to it, I am serving the community, not the other way around.

That means, if there is a policy issue we need to address, my job is to offer the best solutions and do my best to sell them, but ultimately giving the community what it decides on. It does not mean anything to be right if you alienate the community along the way. To build relationships with the community, a school leader needs to give them a voice and provide the type of programming the community wants.

IT DOES NOT MEAN ANYTHING TO BE RIGHT IF YOU ALIENATE THE COMMUNITY ALONG THE WAY.

None of this is to suggest that school leaders should ever do anything illegal or unethical. If a popular school employee is accused of having an inappropriate relationship with a student, a school leader must investigate. This might mean putting a school person on leave, and it may mean terminating a popular employee. My dissertation research showed me that school employees who prey on students go out of their way to build a strong public persona so that when accusations come to light, the community often believes the predator over the victim. If three hundred people come to your board meeting demanding you to retain an employee who has engaged in misconduct, you have a moral and legal obligation to make the difficult decision and go against the crowd.

Likewise, an issue that you will die on the hill for might cause you to go against the crowd. For example, I am one who staunchly opposes arming teachers. If I ever worked in a school district in which the community overwhelmingly supported arming teachers to the point that community members were coming to board meetings to state their case, I would likely resign my employment and look for a school district that more closely matches my own values.

I once heard of a superintendent interviewing for a new job with a community focus group, and one of the community members asked, "What will you do to keep the undesirables from moving into our town?" The superintendent, recognizing the racist undertones of the question, left the interview and pulled his name from consideration. He told the group that he did not want to work in a community that espoused those values. He was right to do so. In this case, the community's values should not be allowed to inform board policy or decision-making.

But these issues are few and far between. In cases of what type of band we should have or how we should align our schools, the community's voice (after proper research and education) should rule. After all, the community owns the schools, not just technically, but also in the culture the community espouses. And the act of a school leader respecting the community enough to allow it to make decisions that go against the leader's personal wishes does wonders in building trusting relationships.

—18—

READ THE MENU OR EAT AT THE BUFFET? THE POWER OF DIVERSITY

A few years ago, we took our son Isaac on some college visits. He was graduating from high school that June and had narrowed his choices to three: Ohio State, Syracuse, and Rutgers. He had been admitted to all and was making one last visit to each before deciding where he would spend the next four years. We first visited Ohio State and Rutgers and were heading to Syracuse two weeks later.

What struck Isaac in those visits are the things you might imagine: the facilities, food, programs, student life, and D1 sports. What struck me in those visits was the reminder that, above all, we are social beings. There are some opportunities in life—many opportunities—that only come through face-to-face interaction with other people.

At both our Ohio State and Rutgers visits, we met people literally from all over the world. While you can meet people from all over the world online, there is something different about sitting with them, sharing a meal with them, engaging in discussions with them. I can't think of many other places—other than a college campus—where people from all fifty states and dozens of countries (students come from ninety-eight different countries at Ohio State and more than 125 different countries at both Rutgers and Syracuse) are in one place at one time.

Being surrounded by so much diversity creates opportunities not only to learn about one another's culture but also to experience that culture. A much more in-depth understanding of another's culture happens when you can actually spend time with that person rather than merely interacting in an online environment. It's the difference between reading a menu and eating from the buffet.

Beyond culture, the educational opportunities of interacting with other people are tremendous. Being on campus with thousands of other students provides opportunities for collaboration in study groups, lab work, and extracurricular programs such as intramurals, clubs, theater, and so on. Yes, people can work together and study together online without being together physically. But I would argue that the convenience of the technology does not make up for the depth lost in the interactions.

Sharing space and time with other people inspires great acts of charity and generosity and community. While we were at Rutgers, students were hosting the fifteenth annual Dance Marathon, a fundraiser for families of children with cancer. Students dance for thirty-two hours (at least, they stay on their feet) and collect pledges to the tune of more than $400,000.

Later, after Isaac decided to go to Syracuse University, he learned his room assignment for his freshman year. For those first nine months he was going to be sharing a room with a boy he'd never met, a boy named Jose Gonzalez from San Diego, California. And I could not have been happier. In discussing Isaac's first few days there, my administrative assistant, Sue, made an interesting point: "You know what's crazy? Right now, he's hanging out with a bunch of kids who he has never met, and in four years they will be best friends. He will be in the weddings of some people he just met last night."

As we wade through life, we meet these fascinating people. Smart people. Good people. People we learn and laugh with. People whose weddings we end up being in. For a lot of educators, Twitter can be that space where we encounter diversity. We build professional learning networks—PLNs—that challenge our ways of thinking and open our eyes to new perspectives. If you had told me a few years ago that I would meet people from Iowa and San Diego and Philadelphia and Wisconsin and Maryland and South Africa over the coming years, I wouldn't have believed it. But I did.

It has to go beyond the Twitterverse, though. We are social beings. In our daily lives we constantly meet new people, people from different backgrounds and different cultures. We need to take advantage of those opportunities. We need to engage in conversations with others; we need to ask questions; we need to show a little vulnerability and share about ourselves. Learning happens when people from different perspectives have the opportunity to interact with one another. We won't grow if we only surround ourselves with what we already know.

In my school district, our students work together on all sorts of projects that raise funds for different organizations or causes and create school spirit. I think specifically of our Spirit Week, our hall decorating, our lip sync performances, our point break contests . . . none of those are possible without bringing different kinds of people together. Meanwhile, technology is becoming a bigger and bigger part of education. Students in all grades are taking online courses much more frequently—sometimes exclusively, sometimes as part of a blended learning model. Students interact via social media, participate in massive open online courses (MOOCs), and so on, and so on.

Certainly, there is value in all of that, and certainly learning can take place through interactions with others on a computer. But what I have seen in my visits to actual brick-and-mortar institutions is that nothing can replace the power of being together, in physical space, with other people. Technology has the ability to flatten the world, but when it is all said and done, people are meant to be together. So how can we encourage and use the value of diversity in our schools? Let me give you a little bit of my district's story.

In 1993, fifteen years before I was hired in, the US Department of Education's Office for Civil Rights (OCR) uncovered trouble spots in our district that they said constituted a "racially hostile environment." The parents of an African American student had filed a complaint with the OCR after their son was involved in a fight with a white student. The complaint accused the district of discriminating against minority students and failing to prevent students from discriminating against others. Chiefly, there were incidents of racial harassment, such as use of the n-word. Some white students bore Ku Klux Klan tattoos. A Nazi insignia was discovered on a classroom wall. Most worrisome to the civil rights investigators was the district's inconsistent policy for dealing with racial harassment.

While investigators found no evidence of civil rights violations, the schools reached an agreement with the Department of Education to correct those problems with the formation of a human rights committee. It also called for a part-time Title VI coordinator to be hired by the district to be an advocate for minority students, work as a school liaison with black parents when conflicts arose, develop in-service programs for teachers, and set up goals for the program itself. A district teacher, one of two black teachers on a high school faculty of sixty-four, was tapped for the position. At the time of his appointment, there was enormous tension throughout the community, he said. But instead of denying that problems existed, school officials worked with the community to deal with them head-on.

When I came to the district in 2008, tensions had reduced dramatically. This change was due to fifteen years of heavy lifting by the staff, students, and community to work through issues and provide more opportunities for minority students. The district trained its staff to better deal with racial harassment and worked with students to help them understand unconscious bias.

Today, nearly thirty years removed from the complaint, our district still spends ample time and resources on promoting inclusion and equality. While the person holding the role of our diversity consultant has changed over the years, we still focus on professional development for staff, learning opportunities for students, and feedback opportunities for the community. For example, for the 2019–20 school year, we are providing varied programming. Every student in grades three, five, seven, and nine will participate in four one-hour lessons in "Respecting Our Differences." Teaching staff will participate in a professional development series called "How Does Diversity Affect the Classroom?" Classified staff members will receive professional development as well through a program called "Reaching and Teaching All Students," while the administrative team will participate in a four-part series entitled "A Necessary Conversation." Finally, we will have one community meeting open to all in which we discuss the work we have done this year and lead a discussion about areas where we are still falling short.

The 2019–20 school year is not an anomaly. Annually, we keep diversity discussions on the front burner through a robust program for all staff and most students. We still have work to do, and I do not see our work ever ending. As long as people interact with each other, there will be conflict, so our district will continue providing learning opportunities for all to keep moving toward a discrimination-free environment.

Some of you reading this book may work in very diverse school districts. Some may work in districts that are totally homogeneous. And still others of you may be like me, working in a district that has some level of diversity but not of what is truly representative of our nation as a whole. Certainly, it is our job to ensure that our students have the skills and knowledge to be successful in college, the workforce, or the military. But more than that, we also have a responsibility to ensure that our students can interact and work together with people of different backgrounds. We do our students no favors if we pretend they will always work and live in the same homogenized bubble in which they attended school.

It's our moral obligation to help facilitate discrimination-free schools and workplaces by preparing our students to exist in them. But more than that, we also do well by our students when we help them lose their fear and ignorance of other groups. This gives them the tools to build relationships with others, lasting relationships that may never have existed without our assistance.

Do you remember *The Muppet Movie*? Kermit, with the hope of making it big in Hollywood, heads west. Along the way he meets all your Muppet favorites: Miss Piggy, Fozzie Bear, Rowlf the Dog, and Gonzo. When their car breaks down in the desert and all looks hopeless, Gonzo sings the movie's most poignant line:

> There's not a word yet
> For old friends who just met.

The world is full of old friends who haven't yet met. Let's do all we can to help our students make those friendships happen.

PART 5

GET OFF THE COUCH

—19—

GET OFF THE COUCH AND OTHER STORIES: ADVICE FOR GRADUATES

Every year, I am asked to address the graduation class at Nordonia High School. The thought thrills me and terrifies me at the same time. I feel a huge responsibility to the graduates and to everyone in attendance to keep it short, keep it entertaining, and give a nugget or two of wisdom to chew on. The truth is, I know that years from now nobody will remember anything I said at graduation; I just don't want people years from now remembering that they were miserable listening to me.

Typically, when it is getting close to spring break, I find myself racking my brain for stories to tell and lessons to teach. I realize that graduates have siblings, so I want to make sure my material is fresh each year. Fortunately, working as a deejay and a camp director, and having ten siblings, gives me tons of stories to choose from. But when I start thinking about what sort of wisdom I want to impart, I find myself with the same half dozen pieces of core advice: your life is precious; do good in the world; write your own story; don't waste your gifts; treat other people well; and be grateful.

But sometimes what matters isn't what we're telling young people, but how. The details matter. So below are some of the stories I tell at graduation to help lift students up and send them on their way. This is just some humble life advice from a school leader, from a dad, from a deejay, from a camp director.

Get Off the Couch

Not too long ago, I got a friend request on Facebook from the girl I took to my prom more than thirty years ago. So the absolute first thing I did was what any smart man would do: I told my wife.

My wife was not threatened. She knows I could never find anyone better than her, so she gave me her blessing to accept the friend request, and Michele and I spent some time reminiscing about the past and catching up.

They were good memories mostly. We met at a church retreat run by the Catholic Youth Organization. We were playing football on a break, and Michele ripped the string off my sweatpants when she tackled me. Don't get too excited. These were the 1980s, when every boy in the country wore shorts over his sweatpants. Anyway, she tied the string around her wrist, I thought it was cute, and we started dating.

Michele introduced me to this new band out of Ireland named U2, and I told her how they were never going to make it big.

I was convinced Michele was the girl for me. We both drove a Ford Fairmont—mine was red, hers was blue—and yes, they are as completely as uncool as they sound. But because we drove the same model of car, I was sure we would be together forever.

One day we were driving on the highway and saw some people pulled over tending to a dog that looked as if it had just been hit by a car. Michele was a dog lover and started crying. She said, "That poor dog. I wonder what it was doing on the highway?"

I said, "It looked like it was just lying there."

And that was the beginning of the end.

Looking back now, that was a horrible joke. The truth is that I was insecure in high school and covered my insecurities with jokes and sarcasm. I had some stuff going on with my family, and I was a little overweight and didn't always have the highest opinion of myself.

Maybe that sounds familiar to you. We are all insecure in some way, every one of us reading this book. Our high school graduates have insecurities. They're getting ready to go to college or get a job or join the military, and they aren't quite sure what to expect. They are leaving the regimented world of school bells, which they may complain about but that actually provides great comfort to them. And some of them are fighting battles none of us know about, such as illnesses or family problems or any number of things.

Adults have insecurities. Am I a good parent? Am I good at my job?

Even superintendents have insecurities. Don't think so? Be a superintendent on a snowy morning. You're watching weather forecasts and talking to police and road crews and other superintendents. And then the tweets start. Pictures of cars in ditches.

"You don't care about safety."

"Seven teachers got in accidents, and it's your fault."

"You hate children."

Insecurities abound, and you wonder how you ever got to where you are in the first place. That's normal. You are going to be nervous. You are going to be anxious. You are going to sometimes feel like you are in over your head. But you're not. You have greatness within you. You have talent. You have skills. You have an excellent education.

And right now, you have time.

Einstein and Edison and Martin Luther King Jr. and Mother Teresa—you all have something in common with all these people.

You all have twenty-four hours in a day. So while you may have some insecurities, face your fears, and take some risks. Get off the couch and do something wonderful. Believe me when I say you will blink your eyes and twenty-five years will have passed.

I'm the youngest of eleven children. My oldest brother, Dave, used to tell me, "If you can't be anything else in life, you can always be a bad example." And I used to be that bad example. Not too long ago, I weighed close to three hundred pounds. Encouraged by a friend who had her own insecurities, I decided it was time to make a change. I started running, and seventy pounds, multiple 5Ks, and four half-marathons later, I accomplished something I never dreamed would be possible for myself. I'm not telling you this because I am anything special. Far from it. But do you know what I did? At forty-three years old, I decided to get off the couch and do something. Don't wait until forty-three to do something. They say that youth is wasted on the young. Don't waste that youth.

I was running one Sunday morning listening to iTunes. I'm not sure how iTunes knows what day of the week it is, but it seems like it knows when it is Sunday. I mean, I may be old, but I've got some Pitbull and Taylor Swift on my playlist. But on this particular Sunday it hit me with Etta James and James Taylor and then that Sarah McLachlan song that they play so often around graduation time, "I Will Remember You." You know the song: "I will remember you. Will you remember me? Don't let your life pass you by. Weep not for the memories."

Similarly, Mark Twain wrote: "Twenty years from now you will be more disappointed by the things that you didn't do than by the ones you did do. So throw off the bowlines. Sail away from the safe harbor. Catch the trade winds in your sails. Explore. Dream. Discover."

Your Life Is a Gift; Use It for Good

I remember exactly what I was doing that night. I was sitting on the couch watching *Seinfeld*. My wife was pacing around the room complaining of back pain. In fact, she kept me up all night long pacing around the room until morning when I finally said, "You know, I think you might be in labor."

She said, "That's impossible. I'm not due for two weeks."

And I said, "Please, just call the doctor before I leave for work."

She called and, long story short, a few hours later our son Isaac was born. Eventually he turned eighteen, and we watched him graduate. So I was once where you are, listening to some other superintendent give a speech, when all I really wanted to hear was my kid's name being called.

That was more than eighteen years ago. Eighteen years. Parents have gone through the same experience I have more than eighteen years ago. You brought a life into the world, you blinked, and here you are. I don't know about you, but that time has flown.

For the students, however, I'm sure the past eighteen years haven't gone as fast for you as they have for your parents.

But I bet the past four years have.

Do you believe that you are sitting here already? Doesn't it seem like yesterday that you first heard your assistant principal, Mr. Broman, yelling in the cafeteria, "Life's a party. Don't be tardy"?

So, as I'm speaking to you today, parents, I feel as if I am sitting right there with you. And students, I feel as if I'm speaking to my own kids. So what I want to do tonight is to give you the exact same advice I gave my own son when he graduated.

There are just two things I want you to keep in mind. Two things. It's nothing profound. It's nothing dying men whisper on their deathbed. It's nothing you'd climb a mountain to hear from a wise sage. But it's what I want you to think about as you graduate.

First, your life is the most precious gift you have ever been given. Live it. Don't treat your life like you did those countless toys you've gotten through the years, the ones you played with for a little while then crammed in a closet only to later give to Goodwill or sell at a garage sale.

Your life is a gift. Live it. Because before you know it, you will be sitting at your own son or daughter's graduation wondering where the time went.

Right now, you are with some of your best friends in the world. You've shared some great times together and have some great stories. Games, concerts, Spirit Week, your first car . . .

I have some of those same kinds of memories. I remember my best friend from high school, Jelly Bean. His real name was Jeff, but once he dedicated a song on the radio to his Sweetums from her Jelly Bean, and we never let him live that down. (I suppose my third piece of advice would be: gentlemen, never let your friends know your girlfriend's pet name for you.)

I remember my first car: a red 1978 Ford Fairmont with white vinyl interior I bought from my sister. One night I was riding in it with Jelly Bean and we smelled smoke. I turned on the overhead light to see smoke pouring out of the steering wheel column. I fanned it away and kept driving, only to find nothing electrical working anymore.

I remember some great times. Once Jelly Bean was out of town, and I had to drive his girlfriend Claudine home from a church group. It started to rain really hard. I turned to Claudine and said, "Claudine, you're my best friend's girlfriend. And here we are alone in my car. It's dark and the rain is falling. Will you please do me one little favor? Lean out the window and try to make my wipers move. My car caught on fire last week and nothing works."

I remember that story like it was yesterday. But it was twenty-five years ago. I haven't seen Jelly Bean or Claudine in twenty years. And all I can do now is think back to those good old days, wishing I had a time machine so I could live them over.

But I do have a time machine. We all do. It's right here in our minds. And we can use it to visit the past and feel sad for great times that we can never have again. But instead of only reminiscing about the past, my advice is to live your life.

You never know when the last time will be that you will see someone. You never know when the last time will be that you will do something. You never know when the last time will be that you will visit somewhere. Savor every day. Never take a minute for granted. Get out there and do something. You'll never get the time back.

The Office had its series finale a few years ago. Andy Bernard said something brilliant on the final episode. He said, "I wish there was a way to know you were in the good old days before you actually left them."

Again, "I wish there was a way to know you were in the good old days before you actually left them."

Well, these *are* the good old days. *Every* day is the good old days. Don't waste them.

My second piece of advice is this: Do good. It's really that simple. Do good.

Understand, doing good and doing well are not the same thing. Mother Teresa does good. Elon Musk does well. It's okay to want to do well. There's nothing wrong with wanting to do well. It's the American way.

But if you want to do well, you start by doing good, by living a life of service to others. You have a responsibility, I believe, to pay forward the blessings that you were given.

Don't take for granted the advantages you have.

You can read, so you are luckier than over one billion people who cannot read at all.

If you woke up this morning with more health than illness, then you are luckier than the million who will not survive this week.

If you have never experienced war, imprisonment, torture, or starvation, then you are ahead of five hundred million people in the world.

If you can attend any meeting you want—political, religious, social—then you are luckier than three billion people in the world.

If you have food in the refrigerator, clothes on your back, a roof over your head, and a place to sleep, then you are richer than 75 percent of this world.

If you have money in the bank and in your wallet, if you have spare change in a dish someplace, then you are among the top 8 percent of the world's wealthy.

We all have struggles, but in the big picture, we are all blessed beyond belief and have tons of advantages simply because of where we were born.

Pay that forward. You don't have to be Mother Teresa. But choose something you care about, something bigger than yourself, and give. Make the world a better place.

Ultimately, the measure of your success is not going to be measured in how much you have but how much you gave. As you venture out in the world, remember to live your lives and do good things.

Forget the Hat: Choose Gratitude

A mother and her young son were walking along the ocean shore. Suddenly, a tidal wave swept over them and carried the boy out to sea.

The mother fell to her knees pleading with God. "Please return my son," she prayed. "Please, please, please, please return my son. I beg you."

A moment later another tidal wave crashed upon the shore, depositing the young boy at his mother's feet. He had nary a scratch upon him.

The mother inspected her son, then looked back toward heaven. She shouted, "He had a hat!"

Too often people worry so much about the things they don't have that they forget to be grateful for the things they do.

We do it as students, as teachers, as administrators, as parents, and as spouses. The problem is when we spend time wishing for different ways our lives could be better, the pretty-darn-good lives we have pass us by.

Gratitude is a choice. It means making a conscious effort to be thankful for the myriad of blessings in our lives.

Health. Family. Friends. Homes. Jobs. Food. Clothing. Etc. Etc. Etc.

We all fall in the trap of ingratitude from time to time. I am as guilty of this as anyone.

Instead of being thankful our son mowed the lawn, we criticize him for missing a spot. Instead of being grateful for having the opportunity to attend free public schools, we complain about too much homework. Instead of being happy for having a job as a teacher, we grumble about having to do parking lot duty.

We need to model for our students the "attitude of gratitude." We need to look for the good in everything. We need to be grateful for what we have. We need to stop whining. We need to be thankful the wave returned our child and remember that the lost hat just isn't that important.

Write Your Own Story

If you had told me when I was young that I would be giving graduation speeches as a school superintendent, I never would have believed you. I wanted to be a writer when I was a young man, not a school person, and as an English major at Kent State, I took many classes and spent a lot of time writing stories, hoping to make a career of it.

In fact, I almost had a story published once, and I often wonder if my life would have turned out different if it had happened. Maybe I would have continued pursuing a writing career instead of becoming a teacher, then a principal, and eventually a superintendent.

In one of my classes at Kent State, I wrote an awesome story about food living in a refrigerator. The vegetables and dairy products had an ongoing feud, but they were united in their quest to free themselves from the refrigerator where they were held captive. The story ends in a glorious moment when the dairy products and vegetables work together to overthrow the man who owns the refrigerator, and as they make their triumphant escape, the vegetables shout in unison, "Let there be peas on earth!"

I sent that story to a small publisher that produced a literary magazine, and the editor wrote me back that she wanted to publish it. She asked me to make a few small changes and send it back for her review. I made the changes and sent it back, then waited to hear from her. And waited. And waited.

Several months later I received a letter in the mail.

It said, "Dear Joe Clark, I cannot apologize enough about the lateness of returning your story, which was being held at our editor's home in Pennsylvania. We are just as shocked as you must be. You see, our editor passed away July fourth from injuries sustained when she was hit by a train." The letter said that the new editor would not be publishing my story but wished me the best of luck in the future.

And so, years later, instead of me being some big-shot writer, I went into the field of education, and now I tell stories about how things almost turned out.

It's important to think about all of the great stories you will have from your senior year: The football team's run to the state championship. The band's trip to Indianapolis. Mock trial setting new records for the school. The bowling team. Science Olympiad. Choir. Cross country. Softball. Swimming. Spirit Week. Homecoming and prom. A student lip syncing to "Tight Pants." There is no way I could include all the great things that happened in one year, but you will remember them forever. You will laugh about them at class reunions and tell your kids about the fun you had.

But here is my advice to you tonight. Don't make these stories the best stories of your life. To paraphrase Natasha Bedingfield, you have a blank page in front of you right now. Where you go and what you do is entirely up to you. The best stories of your life, the stories that your children's children will tell about you, are still unwritten.

You are in control of the stories you write the rest of your lives. Make them extraordinary. No great story ever starts with "I was sitting on the couch watching TV." Take the skills you learned here at school, take the work ethic, take the pride, take the grit and determination, and create a story of your life that is incredible.

And remember to write your own story; don't have it written for you. You are in control of where you go the rest of your life. People may try to make decisions for you. People may throw up roadblocks. People may tell you that you aren't smart enough or strong enough or fast enough or talented enough. Ignore them. You *are* enough. The world is full of cynical people who thrive on watching other people fail. Don't let them deter you. And don't let them write your story for you.

Two more things to add to this message. First, remember that as you write your own story, everybody else will be writing their own stories. And you will be a character in the stories of everybody you meet. How they describe you will be up to you. Will they describe you as kind, caring, and compassionate? Will they describe you as arrogant and mean? It's your call. Treat people with kindness. The golden rule says that you should treat people as you would like to be treated. But remember the platinum rule: treat everybody as *they* would like to be treated.

Finally, remember that everybody has a story you know nothing about. You are sitting with classmates who have been abused or neglected, classmates who have faced horrible illnesses, classmates who have experienced the death of loved ones. Everybody here is fighting a battle that you know nothing about.

The Three Daves

My parents were married on June 25, 1955. On March 25, 1956 (nine months to the day after my parents' wedding), my brother Dave was born. In 1957, my sister Karen; 1958, Perry; 1959, Chris; 1960, Kim. Then my parents slowed down for a while and only had six more of us over the next ten years. I was last, born in 1970, the youngest of eleven.

So when you are the youngest of eleven, as you might expect, your parents are tired. They have other things on their mind, and it is easy to get lost in the shuffle.

For example, I missed my first ever day of school. I went to Dunbar Elementary School in Tallmadge for kindergarten, and I was assigned to the afternoon class. On the first day of school, I stood at the end of my driveway waiting for the bus . . . and waiting . . . and waiting. And it never came. My mom called the bus garage and realized I was actually scheduled for morning kindergarten. One day in, and my chance at perfect attendance was already flushed down the toilet.

But the next day, I tried again. I got up early, and sure enough, the bus came to take me to school. When I arrived at school, I was quickly overwhelmed. All the other kids knew exactly what to do, where to put their stuff, where to sit. They all knew each other's names and were laughing and playing with one another. And here I was, a four-year-old (I wouldn't turn five for another month) who had no idea who or what anything was. I felt so out of place.

To make things worse, this one red-haired kid—whose name I would later learn was Dave Varga—had drawn this incredible picture of a dinosaur. It was absolutely amazing. I had never seen such

THE CLARK FAMILY, back row from left, Karen, Mr. Clark holding Paul, Mrs. Clark, holding Joseph, and David. Center, Kim, Perry, Patty, Christopher. Front, Michael, Kelly, and Steve.

a beautiful dinosaur in my life. It looked so real and had so many colors. I actually remember thinking to myself, "Oh my God, I am so over my head here. I do not belong in kindergarten. I can't draw a dinosaur like that. How am I ever going to make it in life if I can't draw a dinosaur like that? Mom is going to be so disappointed in me."

This is how much better at art Dave was than me. In third grade I drew this picture of a bird in art class using only a red crayon. Red body, red beak, red feet, red eyes. I got a C-. My oldest brother, Dave—who was fifteen years older than me—always had a saying: "If you can't be anything else in life, be a bad example." When I showed Dave my solid red bird, with a solid red C-, Dave gave me some bad advice: go tell your teacher that your brother thinks she has no taste

in art. So the next day, I did. That did not go over well. And when I got home, my mom made sure my butt was as red as my bird.

So anyway, the other Dave—Dave Varga—had drawn such an awesome dinosaur that I was distraught for the rest of my school career. I spent most of kindergarten just sitting by myself at the music center, listening to the song "Rhinestone Cowboy" by Glen Campbell on a record player with those big headphones, over and over and over. Mr. Campbell was singing about making it big in the music business, about being where the lights are shining on him, about being so famous that he was getting cards and letters from people he doesn't even know. It sounded exactly like the kind of thing that can happen to people who don't miss their first day of kindergarten.

I then spent the next eight years struggling at a Catholic school, where Sr. Shirley sent me to the hall for saying I hate math, and Mr. Yeager kicked me off the safety patrol for extortion, and Mrs. Anderson gave me a week's detention for throwing paper airplanes with hatpins sticking out of the front of them.

Then, in ninth grade, I went back to Tallmadge for high school. In my Spanish class was this red-haired kid. His book cover had all sorts of awesome doodles on it, and I quickly realized who this was. "You're Dave," I said. "We were in kindergarten together. You drew an awesome dinosaur on the second day of school."

"Yes," he said. "And also we go to the same church and have gone to Mass together every Sunday for the past eight years."

Sometimes I am not the most observant person.

But it turns out Dave was a genius. First, he was a brilliant artist. You know how you guys have the Skin Squad at football games, and don't wear shirts, and paint GO KNIGHTS on your chests? Well, in my day we had the Bleacher Bums. We all wore white coveralls that we decorated. I had no talent, so I asked Dave to make mine. Check it out.

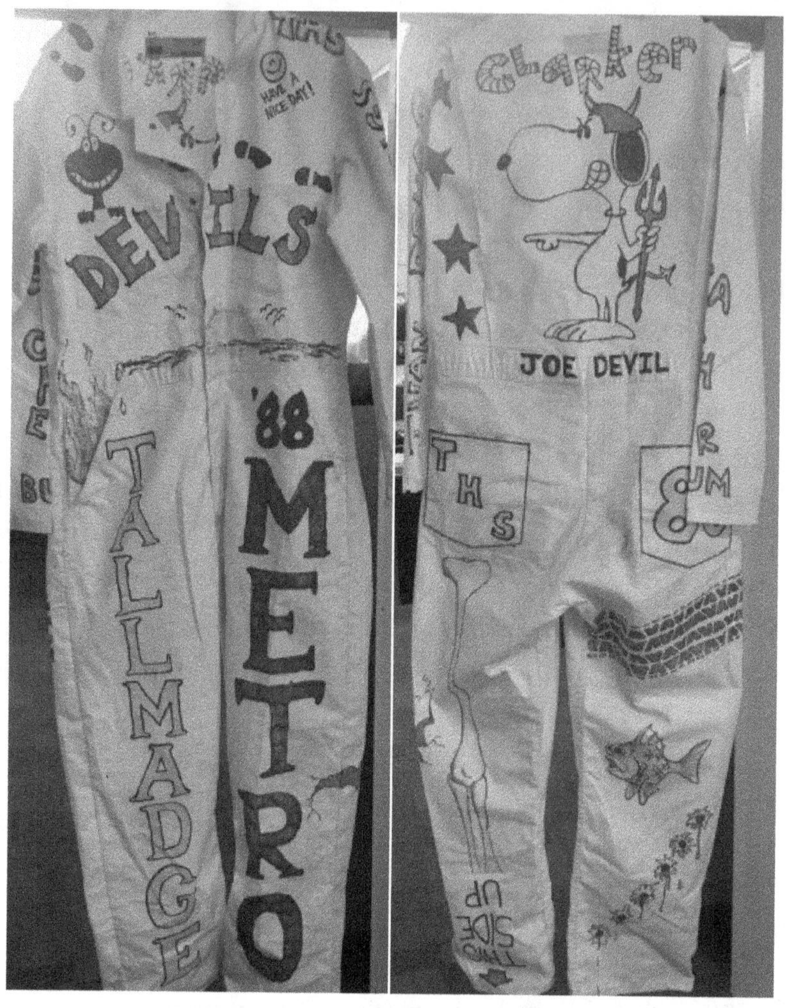

In addition to art, Dave took four years of Spanish and four years of Russian. One time he was at the chalkboard writing a sentence in Spanish, and when he got to the end of the blackboard, he started writing backward in the other direction, so that if the blackboard was glass and you were on the other side, you could read it.

Dave was killed in a car accident about nine months after graduation. He was not drinking. But he was speeding, and he was not wearing his seat belt. But that is not why I am telling you about him. I'm telling you about him because when I saw his awesome dinosaur,

I went into a "Rhinestone Cowboy" cocoon. Seeing Dave's greatness made me doubt my own. I didn't realize then that Dave's being a genius did not mean that I was any less of a person.

Soon you will be done with high school forever. I know you are excited about that, but I am guessing you have a little fear, too. Soon you'll be starting college or a job or entering the military, and you may find yourself thinking, "I can't draw a dinosaur," while comparing yourself to everyone who can. But what I want you to know is you don't have to draw a great dinosaur to be a great person. What you have to do is take the gifts and talents you have and do everything you can to develop those to the best of your ability.

You may have heard it said that "Everyone is a genius, but if you judge a fish by its ability to climb a tree, it will live its whole life believing that it is stupid." Every one of you has something that you are awesome at. It might be art. It might be math. You might be a great musician, or an actor, or maybe you can fix cars or counsel friends in need. It could be anything. Don't waste your gifts, and never doubt yourself. Figure out what it is that you can do, and then do it.

Now let's talk about that other Dave, Dave Clark, my brother, the brother who told me to tell my teacher she had no taste in art. Dave once hit me in the head with a sledgehammer. That was an accident. He also made me scrub our shower using my toothbrush. That was on purpose.

My brother Dave is now a teacher. But before that, he worked for my dad, who owned a small rubber company. Now, all families have "stuff." To give you a brief glimpse into my family's stuff, my dad fired my brother Dave—his oldest son—from the rubber company. Thanksgiving that year was interesting.

But let me tell you this about my brother Dave, the guy who once pinned me down on our kitchen table and shoved lime Jell-O down my pants. As my dad grew older and less able to get around, my brother Dave was at his house all the time, mowing his huge lawn, or fixing his tractors, or feeding his chickens, or working on the tons of issues with my dad's pond.

And when my dad was hospitalized or in assisted living for the last eight months or so of his life, Dave was always there visiting, keeping my dad company and telling him he loved him. So for a guy who says, "If you can't be anything else in life, be a bad example," Dave is a pretty good example. He's an example of the importance of forgiveness, and he's an example of the importance of serving others.

Most of you are going to go on to be incredibly successful. You'll have great jobs and be leaders of your communities. But none of that will be as important as how you treat other people. As you go through life, remember to forgive those who hurt you, and help those who need it. That's a lesson I learned from my brother Dave.

And because we are talking about Daves, let's talk about one more: Dave Broman.

Dave Broman is one of our high school's assistant principals. Our students have the opportunity over the four years of high school to be with one of the happiest people on earth. You will not find another person in the world who loves life as much as Mr. Broman. I would bet not a single student has ever seen Mr. Broman in a bad mood. Even if he was suspending you, you always knew he cared.

Mr. Broman genuinely appreciates all gifts in life. And I am friends with Mr. Broman; I know he's had tough times in life, I know he's suffered loss, I know he's dealt with all kinds of stuff like we all do. But I have never once heard him complain, and I have never heard him say a mean word to anyone.

Mr. Broman also is a great role model in how he lives his life. He's early to bed and early to rise; he loves his AC/DC, but he doesn't live a rock 'n' roll lifestyle. He even eats healthy. I have been to dinner with him many times, and when I am ordering a double cheeseburger, Mr. Broman is keeping healthy and asking for a salad or a box of raisins or something like that.

If I have learned anything from Mr. Broman, it is to be grateful for the gifts in my life and for my life itself. Mr. Broman is grateful for every day, and he lives every day with a positive attitude.

As students get ready to enter life after high school, my advice for you is to live like the three Daves. Use the talents you have been given without fear like Dave Varga. Be forgiving and care for one another like Dave Clark. And appreciate the gifts you have been given and show gratitude like Dave Broman.

Be Kind to Everyone: They Might Become Your Boss

There is a teacher named Mr. Yeager who taught math at the middle school in our school system. Mr. Yeager actually began his teaching career in the early 1980s at Annunciation School in Akron, where I was one of his first students.

He used to write notes home every week to three or four kids who did really well. His handwriting was very distinctive, all caps, neat and straight.

It was the same handwriting he used when he wrote this note to my parents in 1981 when I was in sixth grade.

> DEAR MR. AND MRS. CLARK,
>
> I REGRET TO INFORM YOU THAT YOUR SON JOE HAS BEEN KICKED OFF OF THE SAFETY PATROL FOR EXTORTION.
>
> PAUL YEAGER

You see, at Annunciation our playground was in the church parking lot, which was across the street from the school. So we strong, mature, sixth grade safety-patrol members were supposed to help the little first and second graders cross the street safely to get to recess.

We were *not* supposed to tell the kids that we would report them to the principal for jaywalking if they didn't bring us some candy the next day.

Looking back on it now, I can see how some people may have considered that inappropriate. I thought I was just being funny, but I learned my lesson and paid my dues.

Twenty-seven years later, I was hired as the assistant superintendent of the Nordonia Schools. On a Thursday morning in early September, I received a note in my mailbox. The handwriting made me immediately flash back twenty-seven years. It was very distinctive, all caps, neat and straight. The note said,

> MR. CLARK,
>
> I RUN THE FOOTBALL POOL FOR THE DISTRICT. LET ME KNOW IF YOU WOULD LIKE TO GET IN ON IT.
>
> PAUL YEAGER

I sent Mr. Yeager an email telling him that I needed to meet with him in private the next afternoon to discuss a very serious matter.

I keep everything. So I went home, dug through my stuff, and found the note that Mr. Yeager had written twenty-seven years earlier kicking me off the safety patrol. And I found my yearbook from my sixth grade year at Annunciation. And the next afternoon, I went to see Mr. Yeager in his classroom.

We sat down and I took out the note asking me to join the football pool. I said, "Did you send me this note asking to participate in a gambling ring at school?"

He turned pale and started stammering. "Well . . . it's just . . . a little . . . for fun—"

I cut him off.

"No, you don't understand," I said. "This note looks a lot like this note you wrote me twenty-seven years ago when you kicked me off the safety patrol."

And he breathed a sigh of relief, and we laughed a little, and then we browsed through the yearbook reminiscing about some of my old classmates. And when we came to the faculty page, I saw that I had drawn a black eye and a horrible scar on his picture.

So the lesson of this story is be kind to everyone because you never know who's going to end up being your boss.

—20—

IT'S A JERRY SPRINGER WORLD. ARE YOU ONSTAGE OR IN THE AUDIENCE?

I took my son Matthew to the Cleveland Indians game against the Minnesota Twins one Saturday night. It was a great night for a game. The weather was beautiful. Indians legends Carlos Baerga and John Hart were inducted into the Indians Hall of Fame before the game. And there were Bon Jovi–themed fireworks after the game.

Twins center fielder Clete Thomas singled to center to start the game. The next batter, perennial All-Star catcher Joe Mauer, hit a deep home run to right field.

Almost immediately you could hear the chant coming from the right-field seats.

"Throw it back."

"Throw it back."

When most people go to a baseball game, they hope to catch a souvenir. A T-shirt. A rally towel. A batting practice ball. A foul ball. Anything.

"Throw it back."

"Throw it back."

To catch a home run ball hit by one of the greatest catchers in MLB history is, well, beyond most fans' wildest expectations.

"Throw it back!"

"Throw it back!"

And so what did the fan that caught the ball do? He listened to the couple of dozen chanting knuckleheads and he threw it back.

After years of fan stupidity, of streakers and trash-throwing rock-lickers, Major League Baseball had instituted a rule that said any fan who threw anything on the field was subject to ejection. So this guy, the guy who threw back onto the field a home run ball hit by Joe Mauer in the first inning, was tossed. He did not get a refund for his ticket to the game, a marathon game that Cleveland eventually won 8–7. And also, he missed those spectacular Bon Jovi–themed fireworks.

Nordonia High School Principal Casey Wright likes to say that it is a *Jerry Springer* world, and each of us is either onstage or in the audience. Generally, he tells this to students who are prodded into doing something silly by their classmates.

But it's important to realize that adults, too, are subject to the *Jerry Springer* rule. Sometimes people want you to do things for their own entertainment, knowing that you alone will need to face the consequences. Indeed, the only guy thrown out of the Indians game that night was the fan who caught a home run ball hit by Joe Mauer, not the two dozen lunkheads who told him to throw it.

As we work in the field of education, we are constantly trying to remind kids that the right thing and the easy thing often are not the same thing. Sometimes you have to take a stand and do what is right, even when others are encouraging you to do wrong. Educators at all levels need to take every opportunity they can to reinforce this principle every time they interact with students. It's easier for some teachers than others, I suppose. English teachers have great latitude in selecting reading materials that show characters who have to make difficult decisions, and teachers can ensure student work requires some thoughtful deliberation about what the right thing is to do. These materials can range from "The Boy Who Cried Wolf" in kindergarten to any variety of novels in high school. Social studies teachers can also organically select content that shows historical figures forced to reckon with difficult decisions.

For other school employees, where perhaps the content they teach is not so clearly related to making moral choices, look to current events in your discipline area in which real people may be facing moral dilemmas. Look beyond your math and science textbooks to find examples of real-world situations in which a person was faced with a difficult decision, and tie it into your content where possible.

Nor do you need to be a teacher to lead these discussions. Custodians, paraprofessionals, cafeteria workers: talk to kids. Build relationships with them. Get to know them. Then, when you see some moral quandary in the news, you have a natural way to talk to students with whom you have built those relationships. When Jimmy is coming through the cafeteria line, it may sound something like this: "Hi, Jimmy. I like your Indians shirt. Did you see the guy who threw the homerun ball back the other night? He got ejected. What a foolish thing to do. Cheeseburger or chicken nuggets?" That example is certainly contrived, but we school employees need to remember that a huge part of what we do is fostering the character development of our students, whether we mop floors, cook meals, or teach physics.

If I was that guy who caught the Joe Mauer home run ball, I am hoping I would have been sensible enough to put the ball immediately in my pocket. The hecklers would have stopped after a few seconds, and I would have gone home with a great souvenir and an Indians win. Instead, the guy who threw it back probably felt like quite the fool for being played by a bunch of anonymous baseball fans. I'm not sure of the profession of the gentleman who threw the ball back that night, but I'm hoping he is not an educator. We need to give our kids the best role models we can at all times.

—21—

LESSONS FROM MY SISTER, A TEACHER WHO LEFT TOO SOON

By now you know I am the youngest in a huge family. Eleven children, born almost every year from 1956 to 1970 (when I was born).

My sister Kelly was five years older than me. She died at age forty-one after battling cancer on and off for twenty-five years. I wrote her obituary, in which I commented, "While cancer took her life on February 27, it was Kelly who won the war. For Kelly's energy, sense of humor, and passion for life live on in all who knew her."

Kelly was an educator like me. She is also the best example that I have of somebody who wrote her own story. Kelly refused to let cancer define the story of her life. Instead, she took control and lived her life her way, by her rules, reflecting her values for embracing the present and showing love for her family, her friends, and her students.

When Kelly was in ninth grade, in the fall of 1980, her gym teacher noticed a lump on her neck and reported it to my parents.

My parents took her to the doctor, and their worst nightmare came true. It was cancer. Hodgkin's disease. As you might imagine, it sent shock waves through my family. With eleven children, my parents were spread thin as it was. Though my oldest siblings were in their early twenties, and some were starting to leave home, both my parents were working—crazy-long hours for my dad—and the majority of us kids were still in school. My parents were doing the best they could, but in any large family facing hard times, vulnerabilities are left exposed.

Kelly finally beat Hodgkin's, went on to earn her bachelor's and master's degrees, and grew up to become a fabulous sixth grade teacher. And maybe it was her battle with Hodgkin's disease, or maybe it was genetics, but Kelly became the life of every party. She loved to travel and never missed a Jimmy Buffet concert when he was in town. She was always laughing, always trying new experiences. She never met a margarita she didn't love.

A few months after her wedding, Kelly—at age thirty—was involved in a car crash. She had stopped at a four-way stop and started to pull through the intersection when another car ran the stop sign and hit her. She was fine, but she noticed that she didn't see the other car coming. She had no peripheral vision. She went to the eye doctor, who ran some tests, noticed some swelling behind her eyes, and sent her immediately to the hospital, where later that evening Kelly had a softball-sized tumor removed from her brain.

She won that battle and saw that she had more life to embrace. She and her husband, Tony, had three kids, and she lived her life to the fullest. Kelly continued to travel and be active. One Christmas, Tony surprised her with a cherry-red convertible, which Kelly loved driving. She was a great mom, supporting her kids' many activities. And she remained a great teacher. Kelly actually kept her tumor in her freezer, and she would take it in to school to show her students every year. It always impressed me that Kelly could take the worst thing that had ever happened to her and make it something she could use to teach her students. I wanted to be like that.

Kelly continued working and raising kids and was doing well into her thirties. In the photo above, Kelly has her daughter Lexi on her lap, her son, Garrett, is wearing the hat, and her daughter Leanna is on her cousin's lap (the other four kids are some of my sister Karen's).

At the time she turned forty, Lexi was in third grade, Garrett in second grade, and her youngest, Leanna, in preschool. That's when the other shoe dropped. At a routine checkup, the doctor noticed some spots on Kelly's internal organs. Cancer was taking over her body, and in the summer of 2006, Kelly learned she had less than a year to live.

Realizing that she would never get to share her life stories with her kids, Kelly spent some of the last few months of her life traveling around videotaping all the stories she would never get to tell them in person. She went to her old high school, her first job, her first date, her grade school—everywhere she could think of.

The time she cut her knee on the sliding board at the pool and had to get stitches.

The time she changed clothes with our cousin Carol in the backyard in an attempt to confuse our parents.

Her first boyfriend. Her first car.

With each video, she made sure her kids had a memory of their mom and the stories of her life. As I learned of her making these videos, it struck me how powerful it was for Kelly to define her life on her own terms and not by the terms of her disease. And I felt that was a lesson I would be wise to learn.

Kelly also taught me a lot about education. She was a fantastic teacher: innovative, child-centered, and instructionally sound. But she taught me more about life. Kelly reminded me that life is fleeting. Every day we read tragic stories in the news of untimely deaths. We don't know what tomorrow will bring. Sometimes in life, we are going to deal with tragedies that make us feel hopeless, angry, vindictive, or negative. But because life is short, we deal with those feelings so they don't overwhelm our lives or our stories. Those tragedies shouldn't get to define us. Kelly reminded me that we need to be grateful for every breath we have and act as if we truly are grateful.

CANCER DIDN'T WRITE HER STORY. *SHE* WROTE IT.

And Kelly was a reminder that our kids are our most precious commodity. We need to give them as much time as we can and the best time that we can. We need to tell them our family stories, teach them our family traditions, and help them understand they are a part of something bigger than themselves. That's how we build a legacy, by connecting the next generation with the past generation through the stories of our lives. Kelly might have died at forty-one years old, but cancer didn't write her story. *She* wrote it. She never stopped fighting, and she never stopped living. That's why, years later, I feel like Kelly is still around.

—22—

RECLAIMING MY STORY

My sister Kelly was diagnosed with Hodgkin's disease in 1980 when she was a freshman in high school. I was ten years old at the time, a fifth grader, so my memory of the whole situation is fuzzy. I know she spent some time in the hospital for surgery, and I know she missed the rest of her freshman year as she went through chemotherapy and radiation. And I know that as my parents rightfully focused their time and attention on my ailing sister, it was not uncommon for me to be in charge of watching myself. Sometimes some of my siblings were around, sometimes not. Sometimes some family friends would hang out at the house. My parents were doing the best they could, but in any large family facing hard times, vulnerabilities are left exposed, and one of them was me.

It was while my parents and a few siblings were visiting Kelly in the hospital when one of those family friends, Jerry, touched me for the first time. It began with Jerry giving me a foot rub on my couch. He told me not to tell anybody because others might not understand. From there, it progressed to Jerry sexually assaulting me on average at least monthly for the next seven years.

The title of my dissertation is "A legislative and judicial analysis of sexual relationships between American secondary students and their teachers." In my research, I read 151 court cases in which school employees had sexual relationships with students. Almost every case went into graphic detail about the grooming process the school employee used to move slowly from a nonabusive relationship to an abusive relationship and about the manipulation used to ensure the victim never came forward. As I read these cases, it was stunning to me how many were almost exactly like the abuse I experienced.

Sexual predators look for certain kinds of families—families where there has been or will be a tragedy, families where the parents are either distracted or unable to fully care for their children for some reason, be it illness, alcoholism or drug abuse, divorce, or any other family trauma. My family fit the criteria because of Kelly's illness, which was overwhelming to my parents and left the younger children vulnerable. Jerry took advantage of that situation and moved in.

My research found in general terms that abusers find ways to spend time with their victims outside of supervised settings. The abusers often give gifts to their victims, take them on trips, and test their reactions to inappropriate jokes and pictures, often graduating from the merely inappropriate to hard-core pornographic. Abusers often tell their victims not to tell anyone what they are doing together, as some people might not understand. Abusers lead victims to believe that the victim will be in trouble if the abuse is found out. Above all, the abuser works hard to develop a strong reputation with adults who care for the victim, so those adults are less likely or less willing to see the signs.

This was Jerry to a T. He was good friends with my older siblings, having met and interacted with them through a CYO young adult retreat program. Jerry was funny and generous and gave the impression that he was acting as a surrogate big brother by taking me on outings—movies, dinners, hiking, to the gym to work out (a favorite of his because of the hot tub and shower)—which was especially helpful to my family during the time my parents were dealing with my sick sister.

Jerry would take me to R-rated movies (*National Lampoon's Vacation*, for example) and then direct me to tell my parents we saw something rated PG (such as *Mr. Mom*) so they would not get mad at him or me. I did not have any say in this. Jerry would tell me and my parents we were going to see a PG movie, but when we arrived at the theater, he would buy tickets to the R-rated film, always one with nudity. I was a boy; he was an adult. I was not in a position to challenge.

Jerry would buy pornographic magazines for me to look at while he molested me. Jerry reminded me often that if my parents knew I was seeing R-rated movies or looking at dirty magazines, they would be none too happy with either of us. In addition to reminding me how mad my parents would be if they knew what I was doing with him, Jerry did his best to emotionally manipulate me in other ways. He was obese and used to tell me, "Guys like us will always be overweight." Jerry would tell me I would probably never have a girlfriend, but it was okay because he didn't either, and he was fine with it.

The abuse most often started with Jerry taking me on an outing and always ended with him molesting me in my home, in his apartment, at his place of work (a group home for adult men with disabilities), in his car in various parking lots around the greater Akron area, and in hotels. Jerry was horribly persistent. As we rode in his car, he would put his hand on my leg. I would brush it aside. He would do it again, and I would brush it aside again. It was incessant, and the knee would lead to the thigh, which would lead to my genitals. The only way to make it stop was to let it happen.

Jerry worked so hard to build trust with my family that they ignored or didn't see the signs of abuse. When Jerry would call to ask if I could go out, I would beg my parents not to make me go, claiming Jerry was too obnoxious or a bad driver. They would say he only wants to help us out, and besides, what would I do if I just stayed home? Some of my older brothers would tease me that I was going on dates with Jerry. Nobody ever questioned why a man in his late twenties was interested in taking a twelve-year-old boy on regular outings or sharing a tent with him or taking him to work out at the gym, reminding him that he would need to shower afterward so he should bring a towel and a change of clothes.

Jerry had a few different places to stay. He had a home he rented and he also kept an apartment in the attic of the group home where he worked. One of my sisters-in-law, who worked at the same group home as Jerry, mentioned to me after the abuse came to light that she always wondered what we were doing up there in his attic apartment all those times. Often we would go to the attic for an hour, and sometimes I would spend the night. But none of the other adults working at the group home ever questioned why a man in his late twenties was taking a boy in his tweens to the attic.

In December of 1987, when I was seventeen years old, Jerry took me with him to pick up my brother Chris—Jerry's friend—from Catholic University in Washington, DC, for Christmas. Along the way, Jerry did what he always did. He began rubbing my leg, and I pulled away. He persisted. I pulled away again. But I knew what I had learned years before, that Jerry would never stop until I submitted. He pulled over to the shoulder of the Pennsylvania Turnpike and sexually assaulted me, then we drove on to get my brother. I did not know then that would be the last time Jerry would ever touch me or that I was in for decades of healing.

We brought Chris home for Christmas and enjoyed the holidays as a family. January came, and I found myself back at school on Monday, January 4, 1988. I came home from school that afternoon and was sitting with a few of my siblings at the kitchen table. I had to go to work at my job as a busboy at a local restaurant in about an hour, so we were having a snack and talking about whatever siblings talk about. There was a knock at the door.

I don't remember who answered the door, but on our front porch stood my brother's girlfriend and her mom. They wanted to see my parents, both of whom were still at work. I didn't hear all the conversation, but I caught the part where her mom shouted, "If he's too much of a coward to tell them, I will."

My stomach sank. I knew what was probably going on, and I felt bad for my brother.

I headed off to work, but my mind was absent throughout my six-hour shift. I got home at around 10:30 p.m. to find most of my siblings gathered around the kitchen table. They were silent. I could tell a bomb had exploded in the home, and my siblings were sitting shell-shocked at what they had already learned and what I was about to learn.

"Mom and Dad want to see you," Kelly told me. I was expecting they were going to tell me that my brother was going to be a father, and I had no idea how this news would shake our family.

I walked upstairs to my parents' bedroom, directly across the hall from my own, where the lights were off. I switched on the lights and could see both of my parents lying under the covers. My mom was on her side, and she said simply, "Michele's pregnant."

It was what I expected, but it still took my breath away. We were as Catholic as a family could be, and this was 1980, when teenage pregnancies were still scandalous, at least in our small town.

But then my dad said, "Your brother said that Jerry used to play around with him, and he said that he might be doing it to you. Is he?"

I said simply, "Yes."

My mom moaned. My dad stayed quiet. I turned off their lights as I walked out of their room. I went into my bedroom, where I lay in bed alone. My mind raced about what all this meant for the family. And the feelings that raced through me came from all directions. Relief that the abuse was over. Shame that I had allowed it to happen for so long. Embarrassment for whatever my siblings and parents were thinking about me. And confusion . . . Jerry had molested my brother, too?

About an hour later, I heard my door open. Into my room stepped my youngest sister, Kelly. She said, "I just want you to know I love you." Then she turned and walked out. That was the first time in my life I had ever heard—or that I ever remembered hearing—someone in my family say they loved me. It was just a foreign concept in my family. We didn't say "love." But Kelly said she loved me, and it both warmed me and made me understand the gravity of the news at once.

The day after my family learned my brother's girlfriend was pregnant and that I had been sexually abused for seven years by one of our family's closest friends, my parents took me to the police to file a report. I was taken, alone, into an office where the officer asked me questions for about an hour. It was awful. Here I was being asked to talk about stuff that I had never talked about before, stuff that I was not even comfortable talking about with my family. Not just the abuse, but sex in general.

My family buried their heads in the sand when it came to the topic of sex. My parents never had "the talk" with any of us, and my dad forbade us from watching TV shows like *Three's Company* for being too risqué and from going to our local drugstore because they sold "smut magazines." I got spanked once for saying the word "fart." Any talk that had to do with any body part that was covered by clothing was off-limits in our house. Sex was a four-letter word. So for me to sit with an unknown police officer and give details about the abuse Jerry had perpetuated on me was beyond my comfort level. I couldn't say the words; I could barely nod yes or no. I just wanted the entire thing to go away.

As we got to the end of the interview, the officer asked his final question: "You're a big kid," he said. "Why didn't you stop it?"

And in an instant I internalized what I had feared, that this was all my fault, that I should have done something to report the abuse or stop Jerry. I was deeply flawed, I thought, and was disgusted that I could ever participate in such awful behavior. My belief was that I brought my family shame, that I was a disgusting human being who was unlovable. And that's how I acted in my behavior. I stared at the ground when I walked. I never made eye contact or started conversations. I constantly reminded girls that I was unlikable, calling myself ugly or a loser, and any girls I dated quickly saw that I was broken.

The police decided they would not press any charges. Instead, they drove out to meet Jerry at his home and told him never to come around our family again. Today, when I see victims of sexual assault publicly blamed for their victimhood, I want to scream. Those who say "If you were really a victim, you would not have waited so long to come forward" should thank their God they are in a position where they can wield such arrogance. But at that time, I felt so shamed by the police's reaction that I buried it even further in my own head, which would have serious consequences for me later.

Next, my parents took me to a counseling session with a county children's services therapist. Again, my highest priority was to bury the story as quickly and as deeply as I could. I did not want to talk about it, and I knew the way to avoid talking about it was to pretend everything was fine. The last thing I wanted was to have extended counseling sessions, so I told the therapist what I knew she wanted to hear, that I knew it wasn't my fault. Of course, I did not believe what I told her, but it worked. After a fifty-minute session, the counselor declared that she saw no apparent harm to me. This was just the way these things were handled at that time, and at that moment, I felt relieved hearing her say that. I knew that meant I could more quickly put the abuse behind me. It wasn't until years later that I came to see the counselor's decision to release me after one therapy session after being abused for seven years as nothing short of malpractice. But at the time, I was happy to bury the guilt and the pain and try to get back to a normal life.

Of course, at that time I thought it was my fault, and that shame was intensified by the police officer who asked me why I didn't stop the abuse and the counselor who said there was no apparent harm to me. And I spent years wondering what weakness of character I possessed that allowed me to be a victim. I spent years having horrible issues with trust and boundaries, and I spent years thinking that I was unlovable, that I was broken. I can remember kids in high school making fun of me because I always walked with my eyes to the ground, like Charlie Brown after the gang made fun of his sad Christmas tree.

Years passed, I went to college, and I became a teacher like my sister Kelly. She and I remained the last two unwed Clarks, and when she bought a house, I rented a room from her. During the year or so we were roommates, we never talked about my abuse. We never talked about Kelly's illness. We never talked about Kelly saying she loved me. My biggest regret today is that I never thanked her or told her what those words meant to me.

What did Kelly and I talk about? Teaching. We talked about our students and our lessons, about how we should treat kids, about some of the struggles we were having with colleagues who did not share our sense of mission to kids. And we stayed up late on winter nights hoping for a snow day.

Though we never talked about it, I was always amazed by Kelly's ability to rise above what had happened to her and live life to its fullest. In contrast, I still struggled with the shame and pain of what had happened to me, and I still felt compelled to maintain my silence.

Over the next thirty years, I went through three significant episodes of chronic depression about every ten years or so, each of those accompanied by medication and multiple years of counseling. The recovery process has been a roller coaster, with years of feeling pretty good about myself followed by years of wonder and self-hatred: Why did I allow the abuse to happen? What would my life have been like if I had not been abused? Did I become a victim because of my character flaws, or were my character flaws a result of being victimized?

I spent so much time wondering what my life would have been like if I had never been abused that I often ignored the fact that my life was pretty great. I had a loving wife, two awesome sons, and a huge nuclear family that loved me (even though they say it in actions and not words). I was gainfully employed with a job I loved. I had enough to eat and a place to sleep. Stewing about what might have been was a fool's errand. Instead, I needed to be grateful for what I had.

I also would struggle mightily with trust and boundaries. During these times of depression, I would see myself as undeserving of love. I would question or distrust those who did love me, which would fracture relationships and cause a self-fulfilling prophecy: I am unworthy of love, so I act unworthy of being loved and drive away those who love me.

Counseling and medication would take me out of those tailspins, and I would do well for years until I would regress again. Other things helped, too. First, my work at Camp Christopher allowed me to regain many of those years of childhood I lost. For seven years of my youth, instead of playing with kids my own age, I spent time with an adult male who was sexually assaulting me. Camp allowed me to see through the eyes of kids and create a safe space for kids to be themselves. Camp also allowed me to play in a socially acceptable forum, to do the things I missed out on during the years of abuse.

I have also found a lot of healing in writing. In fact, my best writing tends to come with those times that I was struggling with depression. It was during my most recent bout with depression, around 2013, that I started my blog, which eventually led to this book. Writing is one of the most intimate things I do, planting newly sprouted thoughts onto paper. It is so personal to me, and I get incredibly self-conscious about anyone reading a work in progress. I want to keep all my writing to myself for fear of what the reader might think. Will readers receive my writing like the police officer received my report of abuse? But then I allow myself to be vulnerable by giving my writing an audience, which often reacts with kind words and encouragement. It feels good to realize that something worthy actually exists inside me.

Finally, my decision to become a teacher was made almost primarily out of my desire to protect kids from harm. I am able to look at the students I serve with sincere compassion, to empathize with them in every unique situation rather than blaming them. Sometimes I think about the fact that my teachers never knew about my abuse as it was happening. And then I think to myself, what are *my* students dealing with that I have no idea about? Having that mindset, knowing that the children in my care may be suffering from unknown harm or facing horrible situations, makes me want to do all I can to ensure that all kids are treated with kindness at all times. On any given day, I may be the light that keeps a child persevering.

A huge stepping-stone in my healing was when I made the decision to tell my own sons about my history of abuse. Certainly, my siblings know about my abuse, and their spouses, and my wife and a few other close friends I have told. But I often asked myself, how will my sons learn? The last thing I wanted was for them to be surprised at my funeral by some distant cousin breaking the news to them. Kelly's example of videotaping her life for her kids is part of why I decided to tell my own sons about my story and why I decided to talk publicly about it now.

Jerry last abused me in 1987, but for the thirty-three years since, he has still controlled me. He has forced me to hide seven years of my life because I am ashamed of what others may think. No more. I'm writing my own story because it is my story to tell, and I am reclaiming it from the monster who stole it from me.

I made the decision that I would tell my kids my story when they went to college. And so I did. Isaac was first. I told him when I picked him up from college to bring him home for Christmas break his freshman year. It took me about 150 miles to gain the courage, but finally I opened my mouth and the words poured out. I told about the abuse and my struggle with depression. Isaac responded, "I love you, Dad." Kelly would have been proud.

Four years later, it was Matthew's turn. I told him the same things I told Isaac, this time on the drive back to school after winter break. Matt's response? He also said, "I love you, Dad." Incidentally, Matthew shares a birthday with Kelly, October 21. And now they share a sentence that has warmed my heart.

Earlier I wrote about my favorite poem, "The Second Fisherman." I talked about how it's the second fisherman's responsibility to keep the kids from falling off the cliff and into the water. During the seven years I spent as a victim of sexual abuse, I did not have a second fisherman. I am not blaming anybody for my abuse except for Jerry, but nobody prevented it from happening. If it was not for my brother getting his girlfriend pregnant, and subsequently telling our parents about his abuse, I am not sure when it would have ended, or how.

But my experience has compelled me to be a second fisherman for others. From my time at camp to my time as an educator, I have dedicated my life to the protection and growth of kids. Really, what educators do is teach kids how to be good human beings. Sometimes that means we teach them how to deal with tragedy, and sometimes that means we teach them how to move beyond tragedy to embrace the preciousness of their lives. And always—always—we work to make sure every day our kids are safe and loved.

As I write this today, I feel as mentally and emotionally healthy as I ever have. I have told a few people inside my inner circle about my abuse. But this is the first time I have spoken or written about it publicly, and I am doing so as a final symbol of reclaiming my life. Jerry took seven years of my childhood, and he made me ashamed of the secret I kept for thirty years. No more. It's my life, and I am going to live it. I am reclaiming my story, just like my sister did.

REALLY, WHAT EDUCATORS DO IS TEACH KIDS HOW TO BE GOOD HUMAN BEINGS.

Dear reader, I am encouraging you to tell your own story as well. Life is too precious to be passive and too short to be timid. If you happen to be in a profession working with children, do everything in your power to nurture them, to care for them, to treat them well. And if you find yourself in a rut, in a place where you are not happy with yourself or your life or your work—that is, if your dance floor is empty—change the song.

ACKNOWLEDGMENTS

In the spring of 2011, I was working as the assistant superintendent for the Nordonia Hills City School District. Voters in our district had just turned down, for the third time, a levy for new operating money. Our budget was shrinking, and we were in the process of making substantial cuts to staff.

And then letters to the editor started pouring in. Community members were writing their thoughts of all the things that we should cut, and one of the most common themes was to cut anybody who had the word "assistant" in their title.

I started fearing for my job. To give the community an idea of why my position was so necessary, I started a Twitter account. I tweeted about all the meetings I went to, all the classroom visits, all the work involved in laying people off, all the late nights attending games and concerts and plays and community events. I wanted them to see that my job was important and that eliminating it would be a big mistake.

It didn't work.

In October 2011, my boss—the superintendent—came into my office and said, "Are you ready to become superintendent? I'm resigning tomorrow." And on November 1, 2011, I was appointed superintendent of the Nordonia Hills City School District. And even though our levy passed the following week, the assistant superintendent position that I had held just a week before was eliminated. No, not eliminated. *Merged* is a better word. I kept doing all the duties of my assistant superintendent role and added on all the jobs of the superintendent as well.

So Twitter did not save my position as I hoped it would. Instead it did something much more profound. Twitter opened me up to thousands of brilliant minds, leaders and educators who share with me new and innovative ideas. It has helped me develop a professional learning community (PLC) with teachers, principals, superintendents, and other leaders who inspire me to be better.

You can only imagine how surreal it was when I found myself in the spring of 2013 at a tiny little Mexican restaurant in Chicago with Jimmy Casas, George Couros, Dave and Shelley Burgess, and Tom and Leah Whitford. These were my Twitter idols, all of them geniuses who inspired me daily, 140 characters at a time. These folks were authors, national presenters, and Twitter chat leaders, and they were sharing their guacamole with me, some average Joe from Northeast Ohio.

That dinner, those conversations, lit in me a desire to get back to writing. And seven years later, I am doing something I had only dreamed of, having a book published. Thanks to Jimmy, George, Dave, Shelley, Tom, Leah, and the thousands of other members of my Twitter PLC, who continue to set an unbelievably high bar that drives me to be my best.

I also send thanks to all my friends closer to home who make me laugh every day with their completely inappropriate, irreverent, and incredibly funny senses of humor. Thanks to Jessica Archer for her technical expertise in the area of PLCs.

Huge thanks to Dave and Shelley Burgess and the whole DBC team for believing in this work. Thanks to Marisol, Tara, Sal, Lindsey, and Laura, who made this book better than I could have hoped.

Finally, thanks go to Amie, who does not appreciate my warped sense of humor nearly as much as the guys do, but who nonetheless puts up with the ridiculous stuff that comes out of my mouth.

ABOUT THE AUTHOR

DR. JOE CLARK is the youngest of eleven children. He has worked as a busboy, shipping and receiving guy, pharmacy technician, maintenance man, camp counselor, bus driver, camp director, teacher, football coach, assistant principal, principal, personnel director, assistant superintendent, professor, superintendent, and a mobile disc jockey. Joe believes everything is a teachable moment, and his experiences have given him many stories to reflect upon.

Joe has twenty-seven years of educational experience and is the superintendent of the Nordonia Hills City School District, located midway between Cleveland and Akron. Joe is also an adjunct professor at Baldwin Wallace University and the American College of Education, where he teaches courses in school leadership.

Joe lives in Wadsworth, Ohio, with his wife, Amie, and the greatest dog in the world, Frankie (follow him on Twitter @Frankie_Dawg). His sons, Isaac and Matthew, are out in the world making their dad proud every day. Oh, and he has two cats.

Follow Joe on Twitter @DrJoeClark.

INVITE DR. JOE CLARK TO YOUR NEXT PROFESSIONAL DEVELOPMENT EVENT

Below is a list of some of Joe's presentations. He is available for keynote addresses, breakout sessions, daylong in-services, and multiple-day retreats. Don't see something that fits? Contact Joe to discuss your specific needs.

- If the Dance Floor Is Empty, Change the Song: A Former DJ's Spin on Making Your School Rock
- Camp Is for the Campers (and School Is for the Students): Lessons for Educators from a Former Camp Director
- The Power of the Popsicle: Building Trust within Your School Community
- Red Bellies, Noogies, and Dutch Rubs: Lessons for Educators from the Youngest of Eleven Children
- It's Time for You to #getconnected: Using Social Media to Garner Community Support
- Putting the Treat in Your Administrative Retreat: Making Leadership Conferences and Team Building Meaningful for Your Staff
- Never Mud Wrestle a Pig: Interacting with Haters

Joe has experience as a teacher, principal, human resources director, and superintendent. He is available for consultation on a variety of issues:

- Restructuring
- Human resources
- Levy campaigns

- Community relations
- Negotiations
- Social media
- Communications
- Boardsmanship
- Leadership training
- Crisis management
- Team building
- Right sizing

Contact Joe:

Email: joe@drjoeclark.com

Web: drjoeclark.com

Instagram: drjoeclark

Twitter: @DrJoeClark

MORE FROM

Dave Burgess Consulting, Inc.

Since 2012, DBCI has published books that inspire and equip educators to be their best. For more information on our titles or to purchase bulk orders for your school, district, or book study, visit **DaveBurgessConsulting.com/DBCIbooks**.

More Inspiration, Professional Growth & Personal Development

Be REAL by Tara Martin
Be the One for Kids by Ryan Sheehy
The Coach ADVenture by Amy Illingworth
Creatively Productive by Lisa Johnson
Educational Eye Exam by Alicia Ray
The EduNinja Mindset by Jennifer Burdis
Empower Our Girls by Lynmara Colón and Adam Welcome
Finding Lifelines by Andrew Grieve and Andrew Sharos
The Four O'Clock Faculty by Rich Czyz
How Much Water Do We Have? by Pete and Kris Nunweiler
P Is for Pirate by Dave and Shelley Burgess
A Passion for Kindness by Tamara Letter
The Path to Serendipity by Allyson Apsey
Sanctuaries by Dan Tricarico
The SECRET SAUCE by Rich Czyz
Shattering the Perfect Teacher Myth by Aaron Hogan
Stories from Webb by Todd Nesloney

Talk to Me by Kim Bearden
Teach Better by Chad Ostrowski, Tiffany Ott, Rae Hughart, and Jeff Gargas
Teach Me, Teacher by Jacob Chastain
Teach, Play, Learn! by Adam Peterson
TeamMakers by Laura Robb and Evan Robb
Through the Lens of Serendipity by Allyson Apsey
The Zen Teacher by Dan Tricarico

Like a PIRATE™ Series

eXPlore Like a PIRATE by Michael Matera
Learn Like a PIRATE by Paul Solarz
Play Like a PIRATE by Quinn Rollins
Run Like a PIRATE by Adam Welcome
Teach Like a PIRATE by Dave Burgess
Tech Like a PIRATE by Matt Miller

Lead Like a PIRATE™ Series

Balance Like a Pirate by Jessica Cabeen, Jessica Johnson, and Sarah Johnson
Lead beyond Your Title by Nili Bartley
Lead Like a PIRATE by Shelley Burgess and Beth Houf
Lead with Appreciation by Amber Teamann and Melinda Miller
Lead with Culture by Jay Billy
Lead with Instructional Rounds by Vicki Wilson
Lead with Literacy by Mandy Ellis

Leadership & School Culture

Culturize by Jimmy Casas
Escaping the School Leader's Dunk Tank by Rebecca Coda and Rick Jetter
From Teacher to Leader by Starr Sackstein

The Innovator's Mindset by George Couros
It's OK to Say "They" by Christy Whittlesey
Kids Deserve It! by Todd Nesloney and Adam Welcome
Live Your Excellence by Jimmy Casas
Let Them Speak by Rebecca Coda and Rick Jetter
The Limitless School by Abe Hege and Adam Dovico
Next-Level Teaching by Jonathan Alsheimer
The Pepper Effect by Sean Gaillard
The Principled Principal by Jeffrey Zoul and Anthony McConnell
Relentless by Hamish Brewer
The Secret Solution by Todd Whitaker, Sam Miller, and Ryan Donlan
Start. Right. Now. by Todd Whitaker, Jeffrey Zoul, and Jimmy Casas
Stop. Right. Now. by Jimmy Casas and Jeffrey Zoul
Teach Your Class Off by CJ Reynolds
They Call Me "Mr. De" by Frank DeAngelis
Unmapped Potential by Julie Hasson and Missy Lennard
Word Shift by Joy Kirr
Your School Rocks by Ryan McLane and Eric Lowe

Technology & Tools

50 Things to Go Further with Google Classroom by Alice Keeler and Libbi Miller
50 Things You Can Do with Google Classroom by Alice Keeler and Libbi Miller
140 Twitter Tips for Educators by Brad Currie, Billy Krakower, and Scott Rocco
Block Breaker by Brian Aspinall
Code Breaker by Brian Aspinall
Control Alt Achieve by Eric Curts
Google Apps for Littles by Christine Pinto and Alice Keeler

Master the Media by Julie Smith
Reality Bytes by Christine Lion-Bailey, Jesse Lubinsky, and Micah Shippee, PhD
Sail the 7 Cs with Microsoft Education by Becky Keene and Kathi Kersznowski
Shake Up Learning by Kasey Bell
Social LEADia by Jennifer Casa-Todd
Stepping Up to Google Classroom by Alice Keeler and Kimberly Mattina
Teaching Math with Google Apps by Alice Keeler and Diana Herrington
Teachingland by Amanda Fox and Mary Ellen Weeks

Teaching Methods & Materials

All 4s and 5s by Andrew Sharos
Boredom Busters by Katie Powell
The Classroom Chef by John Stevens and Matt Vaudrey
The Collaborative Classroom by Trevor Muir
Copyrighteous by Diana Gill
Ditch That Homework by Matt Miller and Alice Keeler
Ditch That Textbook by Matt Miller
Don't Ditch That Tech by Matt Miller, Nate Ridgway, and Angelia Ridgway
EDrenaline Rush by John Meehan
Educated by Design by Michael Cohen, The Tech Rabbi
The EduProtocol Field Guide by Marlena Hebern and Jon Corippo
The EduProtocol Field Guide: Book 2 by Marlena Hebern and Jon Corippo
Instant Relevance by Denis Sheeran
LAUNCH by John Spencer and A.J. Juliani
Make Learning MAGICAL by Tisha Richmond

Pure Genius by Don Wettrick
The Revolution by Darren Ellwein and Derek McCoy
Shift This! by Joy Kirr
Skyrocket Your Teacher Coaching by Michael Cary Sonbert
Spark Learning by Ramsey Musallam
Sparks in the Dark by Travis Crowder and Todd Nesloney
Table Talk Math by John Stevens
The Wild Card by Hope and Wade King
The Writing on the Classroom Wall by Steve Wyborney

Children's Books

Beyond Us by Aaron Polansky
Cannonball In by Tara Martin
Dolphins in Trees by Aaron Polansky
I Want to Be a Lot by Ashley Savage
The Princes of Serendip by Allyson Apsey
The Wild Card Kids by Hope and Wade King
Zom-Be a Design Thinker by Amanda Fox

CPSIA information can be obtained
at www.ICGtesting.com
Printed in the USA
FSHW022213081120

9 781951 600303